Best Friends

For thousands of years, people have kept animals as pets. The most common pets are dogs, cats, fish, canaries, and parakeets. Many pets, such as rescue dogs and watchdogs, can perform work for people. Cats control rodents. Some people raise livestock as pets, such as lambs, ducks, and even pigs. Most wild animals do not make good pets, and many states regulate the capture and care of these animals.

Think About It!

What would the perfect pet look like? How would it act?

Veterinarians are doctors who treat animals. Veterinarians can work at animal hospitals, animal shelters, zoos, and universities.

```
Y W Y C K G
P B R H R D A F L G
T P A R A K E E T C O H
W N I U V B S T Y D L C M
G L E S F H J B L P E D A E
U G U I N E A P I G V F N F
P H B V S A L B G T N I A P
P M A C A W K C S H M S R H
Y V F M O N K E Y C T H Y I
K W P B S L O V E B I R D J
A T U R T L E D N Z J N L
V M P L C E B W O T P M
S Y M H O R S E G L
H W N K V F J B
A E
```

How many of each type of animal are listed in the puzzle?

1. birds _____

2. mammals _____

3. fish _____

4. reptiles _____

- ~~canary~~
- ~~cat~~
- ~~dog~~
- ~~goldfish~~
- guinea pig
- guppy
- hamster
- horse
- lovebird
- macaw
- monkey
- myna
- parakeet
- rabbit
- snake
- turtle

SEE GLOSSARY

Furry Critters

All mammals are alike in five important ways. Mammals have hair on their bodies for part or all of their lives. They also have large, well-developed brains. Mammals are **warm-blooded**. The temperature of their bodies stays about the same no matter how warm or cool the weather. Mammals care for their young. They protect them and teach them the skills they will need to live on their own. Mother mammals feed milk from their own bodies to their young.

SEE GLOSSARY · SEE GLOSSARY

```
        D K A S
      C G J B G L N U
    X M F W S X I C T Y S
  D L B K I J O F R S D C D
  W E G Y N S F H L A M V A
  P F C L V B A T V D F S T T
M G K S Q E U B X P L F B U J
U D M D O L P H I N R E W C
S Y D R O C X I H M S X R H D
J W A L R U S J T A K T M J O
P J W R G S K M O N K E Y X R A K I
X F L A K C E B N H T R L I H S P Y L
R M S D O G L I V S K U N K M E E O
Y A N S V F J D M G O A T H S C N
H C L N              O D J
P C U                R E P
Y Q O Y              U E B
R T O                H R
A S G N              Y P W
```

ape	dog	goat	raccoon
bat	dolphin	horse	skunk
cat	elephant	monkey	walrus
deer	giraffe	mouse	wolf

Answer each clue with a mammal from the word search.
Then write the letters in the boxes.

A. I can swing in trees using my tail. _____

B. My face is marked like a bandit. _____

C. I make clicking sounds underwater. _____

D. I am the largest land animal. _____

E. I am the tallest land animal. _____

F. You might mistake me for a flying mouse. _____

G. I like to float on ice. _____

H. I am the only animal with bones called antlers. _____

Going Buggy

Both people and insects are animals, but they differ in many ways. Insects have a hard outside shell instead of bones. Insects have six legs, and most adult insects have wings.

An insect's body has three parts. The head has eyes, **antennae** (an-**ten**-ee), and the parts that eat. The **thorax** is behind the head. The wings and legs are connected to the thorax. The **abdomen** is the tail end. Some insects, such as bees, have a stinger on the end of the abdomen.

Think About It!

Design an insect that could live underwater.

Fireflies and other insects are luminescent, which means they give off light. A chemical reaction in the bug's abdomen creates the flashing or glowing light.

Label the insect parts below.
Use the words in the box to help you.

abdomen
antennae
eye
head
legs
thorax
wings

SEE GLOSSARY
SEE GLOSSARY

4

One of the largest insects is the Goliath beetle. It can grow to four inches long.

One of the smallest insects is the fairy fly. It can hardly be seen with the naked eye.

ant
bee
beetle
butterfly
cicada
cockroach
cricket
dragonfly
firefly
fly
grasshopper
katydid
ladybug
mayfly
mosquito
moth
termite
wasp

SEE GLOSSARY · SEE GLOSSARY

```
        B C A M
      B F T M V I F I Y B
    B C U Y L G O U C Q C J H Y
    F D R C J G Y D S W A S P D B N
    L O N I V L R T E B Q T D I F U F T
    P E Y M C B H A E H V S U Y A S T J B
    G A N T K X K S D T E R F I F Y T T N M
    S B J H F E V F S T Y F G H Y T H E J K B
    T L C K M T Y N H X R B I L G K O R V D E
    V H D C O C K R O A C H U F D U J F N Y E
    N I S R T T G K P W F V H G J G K L F A K T
    W G H N H I F W P L Y C K M L A T Y P R H E
    P M B D I B U I E T J S M M A M D M I B U
    F C E B L S D R A G O N F L Y N Y W K C
    I Y T E R M I T E D E F E O U F G T I
    P B J T X T H P F V S T H T P L H Y
    M N S L H O D I L B I F B H J Y
    O Y D E L K A T Y D I D R
      S T F H R I F S K
```

There are at least four times as many kinds of insects today as all other kinds of animals combined!

A cricket's "ears" are located on its front legs.

Slime and Scales

Think About It!

What kinds of reptiles and amphibians live near you? Why do you think they live in your area?

Reptiles and amphibians are **cold-blooded** animals, which means that their body temperature varies with their surroundings. Like many animals, reptiles and amphibians have backbones.

Amphibians include frogs, toads, salamanders, and caecilians. Most amphibians spend the beginning of their lives in water, and then live on land as adults. They have smooth, moist skin without scales.

Reptiles have overlapping scales that make their skin dry and rough. Some reptiles are snakes, lizards, turtles, crocodiles, and tuataras.

alligator
bullfrog
crocodile
frog
gecko
iguana
lizard
newt
salamander
skink
snake
toad
tortoise
tuatara
turtle

SEE GLOSSARY · SEE GLOSSARY

Reptiles and amphibians live on every continent except Antarctica. In hot climates, they stay in the shade or are active at night. To survive cold winters, many species hibernate.

```
            A T B G C W K
        I G U A N A V G X U B H I C V
      V E V S F H S W C O E U L C S W R T C
    D I L T A I K D K D N A S C H L D N O S A H
    E M D E K L E S N I E F G I R K I F T A H E S
    F A L S A L A M A N D E R F J B O E R Y K J H
    G Q K I G I W H G K H G M O G T R S T O G E K
    H R T H Z G D E Y H G E K T G Y O T K E G X
    A U R J A N G R K W M V K B X I A R T Y
    N S A J C T R J C R O C O D I L E J D U G J I
    K W K T F G O K D Y P L D S T U H O K W R K H B
    B L F A M L R Y A Q F L H E O N L M L E T L F J T
    M T O R T O I S E J K Y N L W M E S F M L A M M R
    S U Y A B U J K       N M O T W N G E N F D
    O O Q O W A           I R H T H K I O H
```

Use the code to learn the names of some unusual reptiles and amphibians.

A	D	E	F	G	I	K	L	N	O	R	S	T	U	Z

1. This amphibian grips smooth surfaces with sticky suction pads on its toes.

2. If threatened, this reptile spreads a flap of skin around its neck.

3. This reptile has spines on its back and can live for over 100 years.

4. This amphibian lives in mountain streams with fast currents.

5. This type of young newt can grow a new leg if one is injured.

6. This poisonous reptile gives a warning before it strikes.

Birds of a Feather

Think About It!

Why do birds fly? Does flight give them an advantage over other animals?

Birds are special animals because they have feathers. Most birds use the feathers on their wings for flying. Feathers also keep birds warm in cold weather and dry in water.

Birds use their beaks to eat different kinds of food. Birds that eat hard seeds have short, cone-shaped beaks. Hawks and owls have hooked beaks for tearing apart their prey. Ducks have flat beaks to filter tiny plants and animals from the water.

Birds' feet come in many shapes and sizes. Birds that perch on tree branches usually have three toes in front and one toe behind, for good grip. Long, wide toes keep a heron from sinking in mud. Birds of prey have long, curved claws called talons. Ducks and water birds often have webbed feet.

```
                              H A
                              V E
                            B K R M P
                          L I M O E R
                          U N W J N
                          E G S H G
                        L J F T Q U J M
                        H A I S U I H O
                      W P Y S C V N I
                      N U T H A T C H B
                      V W O S E A G U L L
                      P H O L D R J W K P
                      C D G O M D T B X M
                      D R O A D R U N N E R
                      W O O B F P F C O I B
                    K C P N B H P E I K L K
                  S J F A M I Y V C K G
                J R T A N R N P I K C R E K D I
Q S G         D J O S T R I C H D W T E H D U O S
W U D L S D Q C Y S P A R R O W N A T I C R F V B L N T
  A H U M M I N G B I R D I S M Z N L N Y R B U H U O
  C V I H S N D T P G O L D F I N C H A J A Q O W L I
  W P E L I C A N         C K         F J M E L I J
```

blue jay	hummingbird	owl	roadrunner
cardinal	jacana	pelican	robin
duck	kingfisher	penguin	sea gull
goldfinch	nuthatch	pigeon	sparrow
hawk	ostrich	quail	woodpecker
heron			

The bar-headed goose is the highest flyer. It has been known to fly at an altitude of over 25,000 feet.

The peregrine falcon is the fastest diver at over 200 miles per hour.

The bee hummingbird is the smallest bird at about 2 inches long and weighing 3 grams.

The emperor penguin can dive underwater at depths of almost 900 feet.

The male African ostrich is the largest bird. It can be 8 feet tall and weigh 300 pounds.

Help the bird find the way back to its nest.

Watery World

Close to shore or far from land, at the sunny surface or miles down in inky blackness, the ocean is filled with plants and animals. Most ocean animals are fish—about 14,400 different kinds. Fish usually live in the shallow water over the **continental shelf**.

Many animals besides fish live in the ocean, including tiny plankton and huge whales. Sharks are fish, but they don't have bones. Instead, a shark's skeleton is made of **cartilage**. Whales and dolphins are mammals. They are **warm-blooded**, they breathe air, and they give birth to live young. Many ocean animals are **invertebrates**. They don't have backbones. Some invertebrates are jellyfish, starfish, and squid.

Think About It!

How do oil spills and other forms of pollution affect ocean plants and animals?

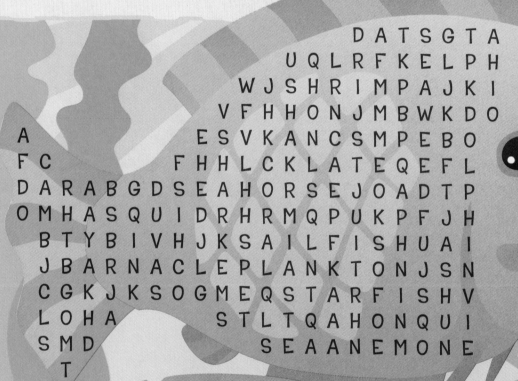

```
                  D A T S G T A
                U Q L R F K E L P H
              W J S H R I M P A J K I
              V F H H O N J M B W K D O
              E S V K A N C S M P E B O
A         F H H L C K L A T E Q E F L
F C
D A R A B G D S E A H O R S E J O A D T P
O M H A S Q U I D R H R M Q P U K P F J H
B T Y B I V H J K S A I L F I S H U A I
J B A R N A C L E P L A N K T O N J S N
C G K J K S O G M E Q S T A R F I S H V
L O H A         S T L T Q A H O N Q U I
S M D           S E A A N E M O N E
T
```

barnacle	eel	sailfish	shark
cod	kelp	sea anemone	shrimp
coral	limpet	sea fan	starfish
crab	octopus	sea horse	squid
dolphin	plankton	seaweed	whale

SEE GLOSSARY · SEE GLOSSARY

10

Circle the hidden ocean creatures.

jellyfish

manta ray

clown
anemonefish

crab

starfish

sea anemone

imperial
angelfish

green turtle

reef shark

Rain Forest Animals

Rain forests are regions of forest with year-round warmth and large amounts of rainfall. More kinds of birds, insects, mammals, and reptiles live in the world's rain forests than in any other region. Many rain forest animals are unknown or endangered. Scientists worry that these unique creatures may become **extinct** because of the destruction of the world's rain forests.

Rain forests can be divided into four layers. The **canopy** is the top layer. A few very tall trees rise above the canopy. They are called **emergent trees**. The **understory** is a middle layer that is shaded by larger trees. The **floor** is very dark because the trees block the sunlight. Each rain forest layer supports different plants and animals.

SEE GLOSSARY · SEE GLOSSARY

WORLD RAIN FORESTS

■ rain forest region

Label the layers of the rain forest.

A. understory
B. canopy
C. floor
D. emergent trees

A **toucan** uses its colorful bill like a flag to communicate with other toucans. The large bill looks heavy, but it is actually hollow and very light.

Since the rain forest is usually dark, orchids often develop bright flowers and strong scents to attract insects. Some orchids smell like sweet perfume, and others smell like rotting meat.

```
T W
O L R         H M O T
H Y E C A P Y B A R A
E M A R M O S E T N A R
T L L G O U Y U R D N S Y
V A E F O P R L T R G I J
G O J P P A R R O T I U E W
H N K S I H U I H U L T R L
T O U C A N R A C L N L A I K
F S C O R P I O N J L O N S
K R L C X M I C G T F A I B
E L E O P A R D P O K L R
H V B T A M A R I N M M
N J R Y H C U S C U S
G A      G R
```

capybara
cobra
cuscus
elephant
gorilla
lemur
leopard
mandrill
marmoset
okapi
orangutan
parrot
scorpion
sloth
tamarin
tapir
tarsier
titi
toucan

A typical rain forest **gecko** has tiny scales and hairs on its feet for good grip. It can run upside down on branches. If an enemy grabs a gecko's tail, the tail will break off. The gecko can grow a new one later.

SEE GLOSSARY · SEE GLOSSARY

13

Amazing Animals

More than a million different animals have been studied and named so far. Probably three or four times that many are still undiscovered. Animals live all over the world—in harsh deserts, the frozen Arctic, dark rain forests, and the bottom of oceans. All animals move, breathe, feed, grow, have young, and adapt to their environment.

Animals are many shapes, colors, and sizes. Even common animals and insects have unique characteristics and behaviors. Some of the most amazing animals are easily recognized by their appearance or abilities. Every animal has developed a special coloring, strength, or defense that makes it able to survive in its **habitat**.

Each of a chameleon's eyes can look in different directions. Its tongue shoots out so quickly that it can hardly be seen by humans.

chameleon
cheetah
flea
giraffe
howler monkey
king cobra
mayfly
ostrich
parrot
piranha
platypus
quetzal
skunk
tuatara

```
      S A
    B R V W
  A Z Q K M A Y F L Y C T J C
  D O F U B J N O M D B H T D T Z
  A E E S E T H C H E E T A H B W E A
  Q F H X F T H T K Q N F S M W F N C T L
  G U A O G Z R G B K U T R E L G Q P S T
  P V H M W A H I S R E T Z L S T H L R H
  I D T B O L N X C I R K T E H Y D A J O I
  H J P N U G Q E K J H O Q Y O I N Z T P J G
  L V K I S A H U R T B K G T N K C W Y K H L
  J P A R R O T L M M V K L I X B L C P J L N
  L W M V T A M A G T O I B U R M S K U N K
  N B R O P N H R K L N D N Y A T H S N C
  U W S F O H H K A N G K O D W F T F O
  T D O L P W A L V C F E P R S F P J
  T K Q E U J U P O I H Y Q K T E
  K X R A T Y R B M R P L R
    I F H H S R H S T O
      F T A
```

Answer each clue with an animal name from the pictures below.

1. Smart Talker I can be taught to speak words. _____

2. Fast Feet I run up to 70 miles per hour. _____

3. Tall Tail My tail feathers are more than twice my body length. _____

4. Big Bird I grow up to 8 feet tall and weigh 300 pounds. _____

5. Ferocious Fish I attack any creature in the water. _____

6. Super Leaper I can jump 130 times my own height. _____

7. Loud Mouth My call can be heard two miles away. _____

8. A Ton of Tongue My tongue can be the length of my body. _____

9. Unique Mammal I lay eggs instead of live young. _____

parrot

flea

howler monkey

quetzal

cheetah

piranha

ostrich

chameleon

platypus

Dinosaurs

Dinosaurs were as varied in appearance and habits as land animals are today. Some were huge, and some were tiny. Some walked on two feet, some walked on four feet, some flew, and some swam in the oceans. Some ate plants, and some ate meat. Some had smooth skin, some had scales, and others had bony plates.

Although dinosaurs became **extinct** 65 million years ago, they resembled modern reptiles in some ways. Some dinosaurs had teeth, skin, and brains similar to those of reptiles living today. There are some big differences between dinosaurs and modern reptiles. Most dinosaurs were enormous, some as large as 150 feet long. Plus, many dinosaurs could walk on two legs, like us.

Think About It!

Why do you think dinosaurs became **extinct**?

```
                    T B O H
                    C C O I C
    R T Y R A N N O S A U R U S N D
    S Y U E E A J E X T I N C T R J E K
    X F A T H P O Y F P F O S S I L G S
    F Q R T P X F Y T R I C E R A T O P S
    M V L O S A F R W S I A T L O T J X T I
    P A L E O N T O L O G Y L P S L R Q N
    B R A C H I O S A U R U S E T Y U
    D E V U A B R S H J Y I N C T K O
    L S T E G O S A U R U S B I       R
    G A L L O S A U R U S M
    N I U Y O E N R H Y R
    H A D R O S A U R W
          V S O N
          J R
```

Allosaurus was a fierce meat-eating dinosaur. Its three-inch-long teeth had jagged edges.

allosaurus
apatosaurus
bones
brachiosaurus
eoraptor
extinct
fossil
hadrosaur
paleontology
reptile
stegosaurus
triceratops
tyrannosaurus

SEE GLOSSARY • SEE GLOSSARY

On Your Feet

The earliest shoe was probably made of hide or braided grass held on the foot by leather cords. In colder climates, people wore moccasins. They were a bag-like covering over the foot tied with string.

Modern shoemaking began in 1900, when machines were used to make shoes. Despite new techniques and materials, many shoe styles have been worn for centuries. Some people in the Netherlands wear wooden shoes. Some people in parts of France wear traditional shoes with wooden soles. Many people in Asia wear silk slippers. In some places, sandals are the most practical footwear.

```
P T C S Y
L B U B L H K
G H O S M I E L C
N O I J A H P Y A N
E S G E N F P S F T C
M R H V D T E N N I S
C H B C A G R R G D E
O S U T L Z S H S V C
Z T I S O G Y N X
W T E J B G H O D
T O V E A K S W F
A N O B L C L S J
P K M D L T A H
T S K N G E W O O
B H N T W T N H E
M O C C A S I N S
E O F Q L K Q
S M T S J D
G R S C
```

ballet

boots

cleats   moccasins

clogs   pumps

high button   sandals

loafers   slippers   tap shoes

              snowshoes   tennis

              steel toe   wooden

The most expensive shoes ever were made in 1977 for Emperor Bokassa of the Central African Empire (now called the Central African Republic). The shoes cost $85,000 and were covered with pearls.

Veggies

A vegetable is a food that comes from a plant's bulb, flower, fruit, leaf, root, seed, or stem. Most vegetables do not have many calories but supply important vitamins and minerals. They are eaten raw or cooked, and used as seasoning.

Vegetable plants are different from fruit plants. All vegetables grow from seeds in one season and are replanted the next year. Fruit plants bear fruit for a number of years. Vegetables grow on soft stems or vines. Fruits grow on wood-like stems, trees, or bushes.

Both vegetable plants and fruit plants can produce fruit. A fruit develops from a flower and contains seeds. Tomatoes and watermelons are fruits from vegetable plants.

Think About It!

What is your favorite vegetable? What part of the plant do you eat?

```
T N A   V A M T     D T N
A R R E M   N T L Q J   B A S Y
B P W O S C X C I T E H K D S T L O
D G O E A V O C A D O F E B F P I F M D
K B R V P R E H B G V J R K E A K B J H
F O M X C B P J Y B L O F A S J R E G E Y K
S X V I S A C E H A X C N B R N A F E X E M
Y T D C R K F U L R G H A K I P W G C H Z Y T
L A I E I N T C L H E I G D V O I U A T U K P
D K M L T G M U F I J N T G R T N S F R C A J
S H P E A M K M V U F C D Y D A N R J C C S M
O I N R F B L B T G D L T I L T D C H O H Z L
X C M Y E C J E M U P S O H X O B I M R I U H
      X A R N W R T B W G N F G S N N A N
      O R C I G N O B E A N K I H I O
      P R D H Y I J W R Y N
      W V O H I M P B Z H
      L S H T R K V
      X M O
```

asparagus
avocado
bean
beet
cabbage
carrot
cauliflower
celery
corn
cucumber
leek
onion
pea
pepper
potato
radish
turnip
yam
zucchini

Fruity Tooty

Fruit is the part of a flowering plant that contains the seeds. Fruit plants are perennials, which are plants that live for more than two years without being replanted. Most fruits are juicy, sweet, or tart, and are enjoyed as desserts.

Fruits are divided into three types according to the climate in which they thrive. Temperate fruits require a cold season every year and include apples, grapes, and strawberries. Subtropical fruits need warm or mild temperatures at all times. Most citrus fruits are subtropical, including oranges, lemons, and limes. Dates, olives, and figs are also subtropical. Tropical fruits cannot survive even a light frost. They must be in warm climates. Bananas, pineapples, and papayas are tropical fruits.

Think About It!

Think about your favorite fruit. Where do the seeds appear? Do you eat them?

apple
apricot
banana
blueberry
cherry
date
fig
grape
grapefruit
lemon
lime
mango
melon
olive
orange
papaya
peach
pear
pineapple
plum
raspberry
strawberry

```
N W A I C
M C D N J H B
S K E H M L E S O
D O C S L X W R P Y N
E L S W A O T R F V I
S I G T P B N Y K G O
R V D T R M I V N R J T
E O N I A C H L H T H U
B I R C G W A T P W K I T V P G I
M P O I J B O J L P L C G O K M O L H P G
D A T E R C E F G U K E N V R Q F L I E N B
W Y P N T L P N R H I M L M J B A N A N A C Y
L M A H G Y I M U R T E M U O R T N R K C D I
I G Y C W O N K F J Y U N B P N H W G U H K N
M U A Y X R E W T G I P R G R A P E F E H O I
E G P K U T A P L R A S P B E R R Y H N L D
E A P P L E P X H O V B T O V P F G M I
Y R G R T R P G R A P E F R U I T I
W C H B L U E B E R R Y W A T O G
E T J E N W K A J F T V H
R E T S A F R U
```

Once Upon a Time

Many familiar fairy tales and nursery rhymes were made into books in the 1700s. John Newbery, a writer, publisher, and bookseller in England, recognized that children have special interests. He published translations of Mother Goose, first published in France by Charles Perrault. During Perrault's time, many authors thought that writing books for children was not dignified.

Since then, many fables and stories have been made into books. Find them at the library, and read them for yourself!

```
        T A
  Y P V C C N B
  P P I E D P I P E R V
G U T D T S F K N I S L U D
R I S T H E L E S T D N K W H E
  A S F D R E T R P S E O D H L
  B I K G R E T J R G L R C I G
  H N R F A P E D O P S H E C L
  I B V T B I S L B U X A W L H I
  O P D B N U G I J Y N H Y L I P
  O K E I G L A N T C S I K M A O
  T J L T B Y X H S T E N K G W V
  S B M T E H F O V M L R P O B M
  L T G A R G O Y U A E N L H S N
  H E S U I P D X B N A P D T R S
  W P T K P A V N D W C I P L T
  Q W Y T M C N T G O J L G I
  R O H X R B R D R Z C O R S
  C S I T G S F E A S C T
  S N O W W H I T E R K
  X B R V T N U E M I S
      L N V J L
```

Cinderella
Goldilocks
Hansel and Gretel
Peter Pan
Peter Rabbit
Pied Piper
Pinocchio
Puss in Boots
Robin Hood
Sleeping Beauty
Snow White
Three Little Pigs

20

Answer each clue with a story from the word search.

1. My nose grew if I told a lie. _____

2. I robbed the rich and gave to the poor. _____

3. My carriage turned into a pumpkin. _____

4. I took a bite of a poisoned apple. _____

5. We made our houses of different materials. _____

6. I was chased out of Mr. McGregor's garden. _____

7. We found a gingerbread house. _____

8. I tried to find what was just right. _____

9. I'm the boy who wouldn't grow up. _____

10. I pricked my finger on a spinning wheel. _____

11. I used my pipe to lead rats from town. _____

12. I found a fortune and a royal wife for my master. _____

Author Trivia

Many books are available for children today. This was not always true. Before 1850, only a few books were written for children. These books were usually based on facts and focused on good manners and polite behavior.

Today, children can read stories from an author's imagination. This kind of story is called **fiction**. The names used in this word search are authors of some well-known children's books.

SEE GLOSSARY · SEE GLOSSARY

Think About It!

Think about all the books you have read. Which story did you like the most? Which story did you like the least? Why?

What book would you recommend to a friend? Why?

Andersen, Hans Christian

Bemelmans, Ludwig

Keats, Ezra Jack

Lindgren, Astrid

Lobel, Arnold

Milne, A. A.

Potter, Beatrix

Sendak, Maurice

Seuss, Dr.

Twain, Mark

White, E. B.

Wilder, Laura Ingalls

```
        G A T M A U S P
    M R B U W Z S T B N G B O K
    I W C A N D E R S E N C W Y D
    T I L H B N T D W M R I K R
    Y N K E T I D N Y L M B L S E
    B U J S N O A F Y A E M D N F
    D K O L E H W K B G M O N E G K
    L L W A U M V O J E L H H R H
    K O C B H S I R S L U N M O D
    J B A L K B S T J M B C T K O B
    M E T E Y E N T C A E I N S K I
    V L K A B L W L I N D G R E N L
    E O Y O M H P N U S T D E I O R
    A N L G N T S K O N V N F H S N
    X O K A O T H W R I Y T G F T I
    P V T E C W E P H K S R Y N S R
    S Y N G A I D Y M I L N E M O X
    R W P O T T E R R T F U G R
    G E A H N S G I R S E
    H N T E P U H
    E S R U H Y
    N P M
```

22

Answer each clue with an author from the word search.
Check the answer key on page 60 to see how many you answered correctly.
Then read what your score means on the scorecard below.

1. The Tale of Peter Rabbit: a raider in McGregor's garden _____

2. The Adventures of Tom Sawyer: Huck's best friend _____

3. Where the Wild Things Are: a dream with wild creatures _____

4. The Cat in the Hat: a cat brings rainy day fun _____

5. The Ugly Duckling: a sad bird grows into a swan _____

6. Frog and Toad Are Friends: the search for a button _____

7. Pippi Longstocking: a girl with a pet monkey _____

8. Winnie-the-Pooh: a favorite stuffed animal _____

9. The Snowy Day: fun in winter _____

10. Charlotte's Web: a spider and a pig on a farm _____

11. Little House on the Prairie: pioneer life _____

12. Madeline: a French schoolgirl _____

Scorecard

12	8-11	4-7	0-3
Perfect score!	Great job!	Good try!	Keep reading!

Music to Your Ears

The earliest music was probably created by voices. Now a wide variety of musical instruments produce different kinds of sounds. Instruments are grouped by the method they use to produce sound. The five major groups are string, wind, percussion, keyboard, and electronic.

Think About It!

Design your own instrument. In which group does it belong?

String instruments, including guitars and harps, make sounds when strings vibrate.

Keyboard instruments, such as pianos and organs, are operated by pressing keys, pedals, or levers.

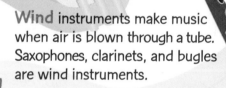 **Electronic** instruments, such as electric guitars and synthesizers, use electricity to generate sound.

Percussion instruments are played by striking or shaking them. Drums, xylophones, and tambourines are percussion instruments.

Wind instruments make music when air is blown through a tube. Saxophones, clarinets, and bugles are wind instruments.

Write each instrument from the word search in the correct group.

String

_____

_____

_____

Wind

_____   _____

_____   _____

_____   _____

24

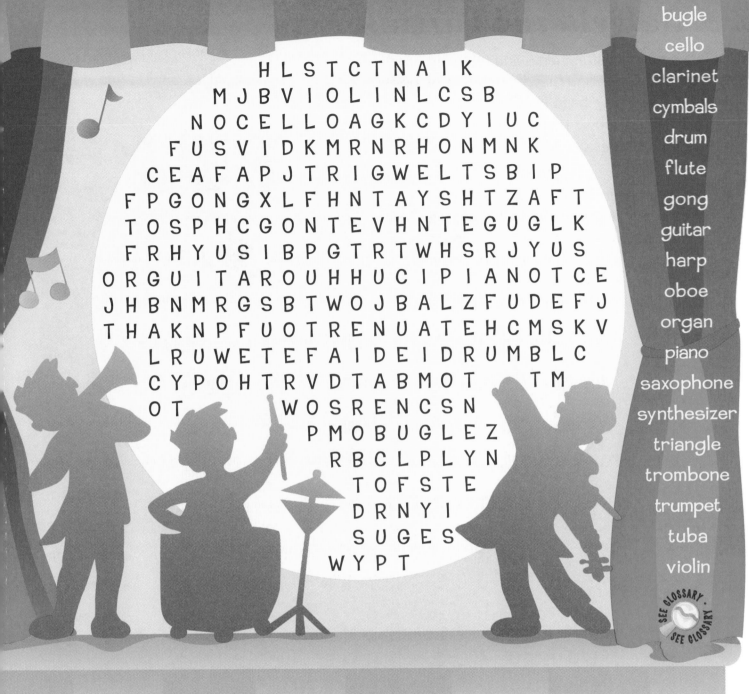

Word list:
bugle
cello
clarinet
cymbals
drum
flute
gong
guitar
harp
oboe
organ
piano
saxophone
synthesizer
triangle
trombone
trumpet
tuba
violin

SEE GLOSSARY · SEE GLOSSARY

Percussion

_____

_____

_____

Keyboard and Electronic

_____

_____

Gadgets and Gizmos

Inventing is putting ideas and materials together to make something that did not exist before. Inventions have been occurring since the Stone Age, when people began using rocks as tools. New inventions can make life easier, healthier, more comfortable, and fun.

Some of the inventions listed below have changed the course of world history. The plow and the tractor have changed farming. Cellophane and plastics have made shopping for food more convenient and safe. The computer is an important part of businesses, schools, and private lives.

Think About It!

What kind of invention do you need? Draw a picture of your new invention.

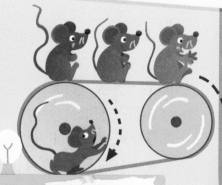

6. The mice move toward pleasant thoughts of cheese.

5. The light turns on, surprising the mouse on the treadmill.

4. The cat lifts its head in surprise, hitting the button.

7. The mice go down the out chute!

3. The gears pull the string that tugs the tail of the unsuspecting cat.

unsuspecting cat

2. The string turns the gears.

1. Spider scares the fly, tipping the seesaw.

Mouse Removal Device

It has been said that necessity is the mother of all invention.

```
      B A A
    T Y P E W R I T E R
    X L J S C M U K O P F L
  D R A H C T P D S H R B O N C
  E T W S C E O E Y I N I T E I O
  K G R B E T L J S A F K N C L M T T
  Y T A I R P L A N E M N T S E Y T E
T O H D P K O O H O B D E I W C J O L A
A R D I G U N P O W D E R N S T X N E Y
W P A O B T W H J T G O N G G R K G G T
D T S C F N Y A F R H M J P L I J I R L
E R M O T I O N P I C T U R E C N N A
G M J I O M E F U P O Y E H L M E P
X H N V X R A Y O T T J S G I A I H
R B P O F K T H P C T S H G X R
A Y L T E L E P H O N E H P
C O M P U T E R H Y T
W G T P S R T
```

OUT CHUTE

airplane

cellophane

computer

cotton gin

electric light

gunpowder

laser

motion picture

plow

printing press

radio

steam engine

telegraph

telephone

tractor

typewriter

x-ray

SEE GLOSSARY. SEE GLOSSARY

26

© School Zone Publishing Company

photography
1826

airplane
1903

compact disc
1982

printing press
about 1440

television
1920s

telephone
1876

Match the inventions with their descriptions.
Write the letters in the boxes.

A. a machine that produces printed material

B. a vehicle that can travel through the air

C. a machine that transmits sound and speech to a distant place

D. the process of producing images on light-sensitive paper

E. a round, flat disc that stores data, music, and other information

F. a device that receives broadcasts of moving pictures and sound

Thomas Edison was a great inventor. He held over 1,093 U.S. patents for inventions such as the phonograph, the lightbulb, batteries, and cement.

Games and Toys

Games and toys aren't just for fun! Games are an important way to teach social skills, such as sharing, teamwork, and sportsmanship. Toys can help develop one's coordination, problem solving skills, and memory.

Games and toys have entertained people since prehistoric times. In ancient Egypt, some children played with wooden dolls with movable joints and crocodiles with moving jaws. Ancient Roman children played with tops, hoops, and carts. During the Middle Ages, toy horses and soldiers were popular. Today, computers create sophisticated versions of games and toys.

Think About It!

What games and toys did you play with when you were younger?

What are your favorite games and toys now?

```
        J L I X O
      T W V E A J A C K S
    H B C S R B Y N D Z V R C
  W N Z O P D Z R A F P S Z H T S
  I E S O F S E Z E L O K X D R E C
  P V F H K T R A M P O L I N E I J F H
  E A U D T U A D G M I K G O H T C A R G
  J H R Z A Y O T K Y L D O L O H Y F D T A
  F G O Z W P H E O N C T B Y N C B T B I
  Z C K L S N J B M Y H R V F L G J O G
  P U P P E T A H O J D E G H E B K   P
  H F T H W E R T S A T O S L T N L
  T C R A Y O N M D B R R L S M O N
  T B S F C O U Z Z O A N D V Z N
  Z O A O G Y P O B L O C K O W T N
  P Z L T O X Y P L Y     R P V P
  D P Q L M G H O N     Z L E
      E T
```

ball
balloon
block
book
car
chess
crayon
doll
jacks
puppet
puzzle
skateboard
top
trampoline
tricycle
yo-yo

28

Sports

Sports are activities played for fun, exercise, or competition. Many people participate in **amateur** sports, from backyard games of badminton to organized softball leagues. Professional athletes participate in sports as careers.

There are different types of sports. Individual sports do not require a group or team of players. Combative sports set one person against another, as in boxing or wrestling. Water sports include fishing, swimming, and water polo. Outdoor sports involve people in nature and include camping, hiking, and orienteering. Team sports, such as baseball and basketball, require players to communicate and work together.

Think About It!

Why do you like playing sports? Are there things you don't like about sports?

```
        Y H J A T
      T B A S K E T B A L L
    G W G C R T S B O V I C G
    H S S N O W B O A R D I N G D
    S L Q K A R L E C T T E N N I S
    F K U P R G U F C H M V O F K T L
  P R I A B C W H S E G O N J O P B T
  H O N S T H B O B R S U K T O N O E
  H V L H W E T O G Y M N A S T I C S
  O O I O B R B S W N H T Y O B J C B
  C L N L V Y H O J L Q A K L A K I P
  K L E Q U N Z L A C I I F C L W E
  E E S S R G V T K R M N Q B L
  Y Y K F N M E W O O D B G U
T O B A S E B A L L Q Y I T E L
P S A T P H W I O P U V K N C P
Y B L I G R K N Q L E G I Q G
R L N C J U D O S T R N G
  S G M     N G O P T G
```

archery
baseball
basketball
boccie
bowling
croquet
football
golf
gymnastics
hockey
in-line skating
judo
luge
mountain biking
polo
skateboarding
snowboarding
soccer
squash
tennis
volleyball

SEE GLOSSARY. SEE GLOSSARY.

Fourteen Largest U.S. Cities

Most cities began at sites that were protected from enemy attacks. Over time, people settled in cities that were along trade routes, most often located by rivers.

Cities grew as new methods of transportation, such as boats, canals, roads, and railways, made it possible to ship raw materials.

Farming methods improved, providing food for more people. Jobs opened up during the Industrial Revolution, and large cities evolved.

Today, cities face many challenges. Some cities continue to grow, while others are losing their populations.

New York was the largest U.S. city in 1900 and 1998.

Population of New York
1900: 3,437,202
1998: 7,420,166

Chicago, IL
Dallas, TX
Detroit, MI
Houston, TX
Indianapolis, IN
Jacksonville, FL
Los Angeles, CA
New York, NY
Philadelphia, PA
Phoenix, AZ
San Antonio, TX
San Diego, CA
San Francisco, CA
San Jose, CA

```
Y  D P I                                            S
O R A H X H E I G                               R   T Y
D S L O D E T R O I T D O P      O D         S T   D
S I A E A C N L S O L H A J C S     C        A X   Y
P F A S N H N H T M A X V I L A K    S H    A N J   F
G H I N I F G T I G G N N G G L G    M L    Q J A
S U I N X W R H O C H H E S A N A N T O N I O C
T H P L D A L A B N A I W Y P I L S I S O N S R
J S O Y A I G H N E X G Y O L S V T O A V J E N
A N U T D A J A C K S O N V I L L E N L I C D
N C F S D E N D E I T R I R L G S T G K H L
J D M T Y L A O T S K J S A N D I E G O M
O N N O L P P Y K C V B N J W K L J N
O X N O H O X R O N A T O C E T L
D I L M C D P N L S S R C
E T A I X F   Y I        S P
R S                      P N
S                        N I
```

Hawaii
The Aloha State

Hawaii is a chain of 132 islands in the Pacific Ocean. It is the only U.S. state that does not lie on the mainland of North America. Volcanoes, some of which are still active, formed the islands. Hawaii's natural beauty and pleasant climate make it a popular vacation destination.

The original settlers were from Polynesia, but today Hawaii is home to people of many ethnic and national backgrounds. The Hawaiian customs of friendliness and vivacity give it the nickname "Aloha State." The word **aloha** means "greetings" or "love" in the Hawaiian language. Vacationers are often greeted with a wreath of flowers called a **lei** (lā) when they arrive at a Hawaiian island.

Think About It

Where did your state's settlers originate?

Kauai

Niihau

Oahu • Pearl Harbor

Pacific Ocean

Honolulu

Molokai

Maui

Lanai

Kahoolawe

Pacific Ocean

Hawaii

bananas
canyons
Honolulu
hula
islands
Kauai
lava
leis
Maui

mountains
Oahu
papayas
Pearl Harbor
pineapples
Polynesians
sugar
valleys
volcanoes
waves

SEE GLOSSARY. SEE GLOSSARY

```
              B
    L         A K
    O         A U
    I A     L O
H B     U V H I Y       Y J
V G L U A   G M A U I   B T D G
  A C M N W V A L L E Y S
  V O L C A N O E S I
  A A P T N V I U
  G Y O K T R E H
  H I L I S L A N D S W L
  F M S N D M G U I R C M
  N K Y O D T N P P A X N K S
  U I H O V U L E I S A I A P O
  X A O P P L N V N U P P G O H P
  T U N F Y A L T E M B L A L I O
  V M O B A N A N A S A R N Y C L
  A S L E Y M X S P I U I S N A Y G
  L Y U U E L T K P O N T W E N S M
  U R L G I S H U L A U S M S Y U
  F U V A V W A E R O V L I O I
  L C O S R E I S B R Y Y A N W
  P E A R L H A R B O R N S
  E N R P T N S N Y S
```

The Hawaiian alphabet has only 12 letters — **a, e, h, i, k, l, m, n, o, p, u,** and **w.**

31

Pioneers

Pioneers are the first people to venture into new lands. Thousands of American pioneers left the eastern United States to settle on land between the Appalachian Mountains and the Pacific Ocean. Two major pioneer migrations are an important part of U.S. history. Around 1760, pioneers traveled from the Appalachians to the Mississippi Valley. During the second migration, which began in the 1840s, pioneers reached Oregon and California.

There are many famous pioneers, including Daniel Boone, Kit Carson, and Davy Crockett. It is important to remember that thousands of men and women faced dangers and hardships as they looked for new opportunities. Pioneers discovered important facts about geography, transportation, and agriculture.

Think About It

Why do you think pioneers left the eastern United States?

PIONEER TRAILS

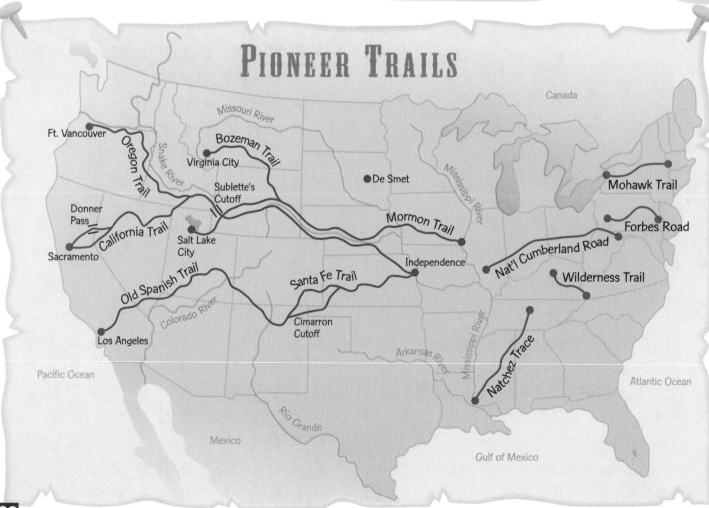

Canada

Missouri River

Ft. Vancouver

Oregon Trail

Snake River

Bozeman Trail

Virginia City

Sublette's Cutoff

De Smet

Mississippi River

Mohawk Trail

Forbes Road

Donner Pass

California Trail

Salt Lake City

Mormon Trail

Nat'l Cumberland Road

Sacramento

Old Spanish Trail

Independence

Wilderness Trail

Colorado River

Santa Fe Trail

Cimarron Cutoff

Mississippi River

Los Angeles

Arkansas River

Natchez Trace

Pacific Ocean

Atlantic Ocean

Rio Grande

Mexico

Gulf of Mexico

32

In the winter of 1846–1847, a party of 82 pioneers became snowbound at Donner Pass, a cut through the Sierra Nevadas. Through their desperate measures, 47 people survived.

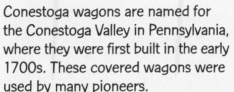

Laura Ingalls Wilder wrote eight "Little House" books based on her pioneer childhood. Five of the stories take place in De Smet, South Dakota.

Conestoga wagons are named for the Conestoga Valley in Pennsylvania, where they were first built in the early 1700s. These covered wagons were used by many pioneers.

```
T E        G H S          A P L E        D T S
A E M D V Q M R P I D X S C R W R E Y F D J B P C M V P G
H P J S F D N V Y B O W I E R D O S Q D S E O N H C W S C
J F P D S U B L E T T E K I C O L T E R R M O T L L N D
E C L R E C L A R K X A Y O N C P G C E I N R Y O E E
T B F E I K A W I V G J K H N F K L N L S E B S U B W
M D W T S T F R F E B S G W E G S E Y H O Y Q T G O G
T R U K E T H S N E H M D R C P W T E N W H A H I
O N S T S E K I O R L E I F W P I R T J I Y L L W
V P K H K M D M J N E Y L T M B S I X O N H R I T
P Y S N B R I D G E R W E H L R W H I T M A N
```

Appleseed, **Johnny**

Boone, **Daniel**

Bowie, **James**

Bridger, **Jim**

Carson, **Kit**

Clark, **William**

Colter, **John**

Crockett, **Davy**

Donner, **George & Jacob**

Jemison, **Mary**

Lewis, **Meriwether**

McLoughlin, **John**

Smith, **Jebediah**

Sublette, **William**

Whitman, **Marcus**

Native Americans

Native Americans (often called American Indians) are the original people of North and South America. There were hundreds of different tribes. The languages, religions, and customs of the tribes varied widely.

In the late 1700s, the U.S. government and Native American tribal leaders signed treaties to maintain peace and settle land disputes. In 1830, Congress passed the Indian Removal Act. This forced Native Americans to live on reservations. Today, many Native Americans continue to struggle to maintain their cultures and protect their rights.

SEE GLOSSARY · SEE GLOSSARY

Think About It

How is the life of a modern Native American different from a Native American's life before European settlers arrived?

Inuit
Iroquois
Cheyenne
Chippewa
Crow
Haida
Apache
Cherokee
Kickapoo
Kwakiutl
Navajo
Nez Perce
Pomo
Pueblo
Seminole
Shawnee
Sioux
Ute

```
A U                                          T A H E
G O Y W H V J                            I R Z U A P E
C C K I C K A P O O C U W A I P T A I R O Q U O I S Y C
C P W P R O E U T K I U F S H U K W P N V C J V D O D A
H A X T C H E Y E N N E W H V U P A W U H A O A L E
X K W D H R B S I U A I P P A O X U I F I U F V J N
G I Q T E Z L X E W V U C W G W H K W O P T Y G O A
U H U R O O N O Y A M E H R P N W C F P C O L H
T C R O W I N Q Z J O A I N O N E Z P E R C E I
L I V K P R T X E O T P S J E L E E C W Y N O
O K E H N I P K W Y A N I X O B H K A E W N
S E M I N O L E D C O L O C B U A L C L
X O C I M W O P H P K W U T E O P U
I U O A H I E Y A N N X E X I
O K F X R J C K I P O
```

Northwestern totem poles serve as an emblem of a family or clan. They can tell a story or mark a grave.

Inuit live farther north than any other people. The Inuit obtain most of their food from hunting and fishing.

Hiawatha, an Iroquois leader, helped bring peace to the five main Iroquois tribes. They formed an alliance called the Great Peace, also known as the Iroquois League.

Buffalo provided meat, clothing, and shelter for Native Americans living on the Plains.

Little Big Horn
Montana •

• Wounded Knee
South Dakota

Serpent Mound
Ohio

Sacagawea, a Shoshone woman, was a guide and interpreter for the Lewis and Clark expedition to the Pacific Ocean.

Mesa Verde
Colorado

Trail of Tears
Southeast to Oklahoma

Sequoyah invented a system of writing for his native language of Cherokee.

Southwestern Pueblo people lived in connected stone or adobe buildings that were up to four stories tall.

Crazy Horse, Geronimo, Osceola, and Pontiac were famous Native American warriors.

Canada

Canada is the second largest country in the world. It is rich in scenic beauty and natural resources. A federal government binds Canada's 10 provinces and 3 territories in a democratic nation. Canada's closest economic and social ties are with the United States, which shares common interests and a common background.

Think About It

Why do you think Canada's population is less than the U.S. population even though Canada is a larger country?

Approximate Area

Canada	3,851,800 sq. mi.
United States	3,717,796 sq. mi.

Approximate Population (2001)

Canada	31 million
United States	276 million

On February 15, 1965, Canada flew a new flag. It showed a red maple leaf, a symbol of Canada.

United States

Yukon

Northwest Territories

Nunavut

British Columbia

Alberta

Saskatchewan

Manitoba

Hudson Bay

Ontario

Quebec

Newfoundland

Prince Edward Island

Nova Scotia

New Brunswick

United States

Niagara Falls

The territory of Nunavut was established in 1999. The word **Nunavut** means "our land" in Inuit.

Canadians celebrate Canada Day on July 1, the date in 1867 that Canada became a country. Canada still recognizes the British monarch as queen of Canada.

Niagara Falls is one of the greatest hydro-electric power sources in the world.

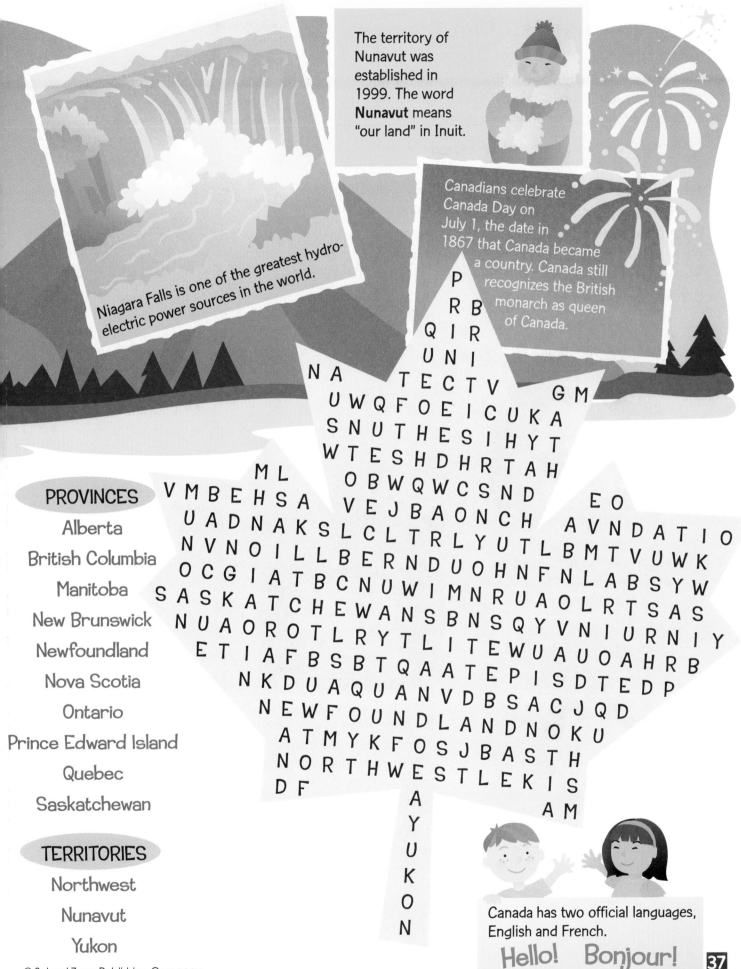

PROVINCES

Alberta

British Columbia

Manitoba

New Brunswick

Newfoundland

Nova Scotia

Ontario

Prince Edward Island

Quebec

Saskatchewan

TERRITORIES

Northwest

Nunavut

Yukon

Canada has two official languages, English and French.

Hello!   Bonjour!

37

Explorers

Since prehistoric times, people have engaged in exploration. Early people searched for food and shelter. Eventually, prehistoric people populated all of the continents except Antarctica.

During ancient and medieval times, explorers from Europe, the Middle East, and Asia charted territories far from their homelands. Many parts of the world remained isolated until the Europeans became active explorers in the 1400s. By the early 1900s, most parts of the world had been mapped. New frontiers for exploration are the oceans and outer space.

A.D. 950–1000

ERIC THE RED
This Viking from Norway was named Eric Thorvaldson. He was nicknamed for his red hair. He discovered and colonized Greenland.

1543–1596

SIR FRANCIS DRAKE
Drake was the first Englishman to sail around the world. He earned a reputation as a ruthless pirate.

1930–Present

NEIL ARMSTRONG
This U.S. astronaut was the first person to step on the moon. He and Edwin Aldrin Jr. landed on the moon on July 20, 1969.

1491–1557

JACQUES CARTIER
When he explored North America, this French explorer became friends with the Iroquois people. The first corn ever seen in Europe was delivered by his crew.

1254–1324

MARCO POLO
This Italian explorer traveled through China and central Asia. His journey totaled 15,000 miles and took 24 years.

38

Amundsen, Roald
Armstrong, Neil
Cabot, John
Cartier, Jacques
Champlain, Samuel de
Clark, William
Columbus, Christopher
Cortés, Hernando

Drake, Sir Francis
Ericson, Leif
Eric the Red
Hillary, Sir Edmund Percival
Hudson, Henry
Lewis, Meriwether

Livingstone, David
Magellan, Ferdinand
Marquette, Jacques
Polo, Marco
Ponce de León, Juan
Soto, Hernando de

SEE GLOSSARY · SEE GLOSSARY

Jeanne Baret was probably the first woman to sail around the world. In 1766, this young Frenchwoman disguised herself as a male servant and sailed on the first French voyage around the world.

```
              B C Y H
        L E W U N I P N L M D
  D A M U N D S E N R O A C Y L W A E C
  R W Q K D C A R T I E R O D A R R L
  O T D U S Y W R N S C V L R E Q T K
  C N S F O L I E M T F T U L T U L I
  O H G G I H S G D S O G H L K E G W
  L S I Y R T I N P M T Y M E B T S F
  U R U L G I W B N A S R T N R T I I
  M E A J L I V I N G S T O N E E V
  B A K C H A M P L A I N R N H K D
  U B G L L I R Q O R T G B B G O
  S V M E A G F Y U Y H R T L N
  C O R T A L C B   N   N N F N D
T W D H F     O     L     O   O D O U
H U D S O N I M U H L E A H C P U A I P L H K
H Y E R I C S O N C Q W T N N A C F Q O U D
N F K A H I A R D U I U M P H B R F L H
K T D S K M H K N I S D S X R S O T O A
    P O N C E D E L E O N T U M F K T I
```

South America

South America is the fourth largest continent. It is almost twice as large as the United States, but it has fewer people. Almost half of South America is a wilderness of high mountains, empty plains, and tropical forests. Most of the continent is warm all year. The exception is high in the Andes Mountains, where it is always cold. The Amazon River Basin supports the world's largest tropical rain forest.

Most of the large, modern cities are near the coasts. The standard of living in South America varies greatly. Although all South American countries have a small class of wealthy landowners, politicians, and businesspeople, most of the population is poor.

Think About It

South America has been slow to develop its rich natural resources. Why?

The equator, which crosses Ecuador, gave the country its name.

The Amazon River flows about 4,000 miles from the Andes in Peru to the Atlantic Ocean. Only the Nile River is longer.

Brazil contains the largest area of tropical rain forest in the world.

Many people living in the Andes herd llamas, alpacas, and vicuñas. The hair and fur of these animals is used to make clothing.

Gauchos are the cowboys of Argentina and Uruguay. They wear wide-brimmed felt hats and baggy pants called **bombachas**.

Venezuela
Guyana
Suriname
French Guiana
Colombia
Ecuador
Amazon River
Peru
Brazil
Bolivia
Paraguay
Argentina
Uruguay
Chile
Falkland Islands

40

Rain forests surround the Amazon River. They cover more than a third of South America. Every day, rain forests are cleared for farming and other uses, causing erosion and the loss of species.

Angel Falls in eastern Venezuela is the tallest waterfall in the world. It plunges about 3,212 feet. That's longer than 10 football fields!

Argentina
Bolivia
Brazil
Chile
Colombia
Ecuador
Falkland Islands
French Guiana
Guyana
Paraguay
Peru
Suriname
Uruguay
Venezuela

```
E C U A D O R V A
F R O D B G C S P
A P Y L M O U U A C
L R Z D O L G Y R L
K T G R E M U L A K Y
V R L U H E C T B Z G N I
Z B G N E A F B G N H Y I U R A K
I S Y R H U N J R Z V T H N A E H L
D C T I U N O Y D E A V B N I F Y C I U
E C H N F L R C D I U Z L E H Z N D L J
B O L I V I A V I K S R I U V N L K A M K
J Y A L Y A N C H N L C L I E A G U A Y
G W F R E N C H G U I A N A V N L U M D
H P G S U Z V A F N D N M S Y M I A N
U H C E O D K E Z I R L D O E V T U R
P D P U R U G U A Y P H S Z H P Y P T
E Y C U B I U Y Z Q H A N Y C B T A Z E
```

Alaska
The Last Frontier

Alaska is the largest state in the United States. It is more than twice the size of Texas. But Alaska has fewer people than any other state.

The United States purchased Alaska from Russia in 1867 for about two cents per acre. At the time, people made fun of the purchase, thinking that Alaska was nothing but snow and ice. The United States soon realized that the value of Alaskan resources was far greater than the purchase price.

Alaska's state flag was designed by a 13-year-old boy. Seven stars form the Big Dipper, symbolizing Alaska's gold-mining industry. The eighth star in the corner is the North Star, representing the state's northern location.

Think About It

Design a flag to symbolize your state.

Alaska's most western point is only 51 miles from Russia. Why do you think Russia sold Alaska to the United States?

Word search grid:

```
S D                                                              C B
E E        C E      Y I                      U T      L Y        A E C
H P        N A      A K              B N      L Y      I P        R C R
Q G J      D U      S G      L       F H      I P      B B        I S P
U H T I M B E R B A    E R  F   I W  B N L    O I L
O U A M I N E R A L S  J A  S G L A C I E R U W
       Y W M           M U S H E R S R Y A
       H M O U N T A I N S T N K M
K A Y A K Y G Y A G N E N T V O R P D
J E M I N A N C H O R A G E M H A
       V S K H L G R Y T F R J
       E T D S T W R N
       V A B I H P M J
       D E H L R Q O U U B
       G O R S U I S N R
       V O L C A N O E S
       L I F H K U B A T
       C M U I E I T U K
       V A V K R T I S
       N O A G
```

Word list:
- Anchorage
- caribou
- earthquake
- fish
- gold
- glacier
- Inuit
- Juneau
- kayak
- minerals
- mountains
- mushers
- oil
- salmon
- seals
- timber
- volcanoes

National Parks

As people moved westward in the early 1800s, the United States became involved in protecting and preserving unique and special places. In 1872, the U.S. government established the first national park in the world, Yellowstone National Park. Since that time, more than 350 national parks have been created. Most national parks are preserved for their outstanding beauty, their unique wildlife, or the scientific importance of their natural features.

Think About It

What are some of the problems facing national parks today?

```
          N C                 E U A
          Y H           T S Y P W H J V B
    C G I R U Y L P C N W S C N M K T
    N K J Y O E L A G R A N D C A N Y O N S C
    S C T M R W A L R D C E R A E N Y K E O H G U
    F Y O S E M I T E B L H F K D S D L A F N E
    I W N G I A L S V F G S O G L D W A E D R T W E G L
    H X G O S D Y N I A L H B V W H E B O L Y M P I C Y M O H
    L   N L O I E V E R G L A D E S A E T O B I H
    S C A N Y O N L A N D S A G T I K Y D E
    H A N C E S A C U K C H O R H O N L K X
    E   G   I V H F G L A U S N V Y N L
        E N E A M V E A C A V R E
        R Y N L E A G W L H J N
        V M A R N U S L O K
        A P C N V A T E Y G
        D Y U S D R O Y S
        E C V R O E O D
        S N H G X A N R
        T O A C H D H O
        B A D L A N D S
        G Y V O I S S V
        V L R W A N B A
        E N O M I
```

Old Faithful is a geyser in Yellowstone National Park. It erupts about every 76 minutes, shooting a stream of boiling water more than 100 meters high.

The smallest U.S. national park is Thaddeus Kosciuszko National Monument in Pennsylvania. This monument honors a Polish patriot of the Revolutionary War and covers only 0.02 of an acre.

Old Faithful

Badlands
Canyonlands
Carlsbad Caverns
Death Valley
Denali
Everglades
Glacier
Grand Canyon
Olympic
Redwood
Saguaro
Shenandoah
Yellowstone
Yosemite

SEE GLOSSARY · SEE GLOSSARY

Buildings

Buildings are designed by architects to meet goals of use, strength, and beauty. Early people lived in simple huts and tents for protection from the weather and animals. Today's buildings are a diverse and elaborate mixture of styles and purposes. They range from simple homes to temples, monuments, churches, schools, and commercial buildings.

The development of elevators in the 1800s led to the design and construction of skyscrapers.

```
C V E A P T I S W P U C H U R C H
A S Y K Y N P I L B E O T C T
F T O W E R W A Q E L S V I S
I N H D L V A D G W R P G O Y
U A E M J P N M S O E I H C N L S K E
L R K Y X L N K I A D T O D A I V W Y
S H W G C A T H E D R A L V G B D E H
H K T H G N O R A F L C N O R I R
D I Y U S E F B M T I U H U G A V N
Y V R S V T P Y E H M P A C U R S T
N K E B C A A M T O O S L A E Y N M
R Y T D E R L D O Y G T L S O L C
B R S T M I A E I D O O E T W D G
N A N H E U N P B U E I N L P I A
P L G E O M I S E J M O O E T U
V Y O D U S P M I R U D S P P A
K L N Q C R S L D G S B N M T Y
P T R U H Y U F E A E R V E N
L H O U S E M O S Q U E T M S
A L X M T M L Y P R M Y C E T
V C P R B K P O N S B K T H P
```

cabin
castle
cathedral
church
hospital
hotel
house
library
mosque
museum
pagoda
planetarium
pyramid
skyscraper
stadium
synagogue
temple
tomb
tower

SEE GLOSSARY · SEE GLOSSARY

Agriculture

Agriculture is the science of growing plants and raising animals for food, clothing, medicines, and other human needs. Agriculture is the world's most important industry. At one time, most people were farmers. As agricultural methods improved, farmers were able to provide a greater number of plants and animals.

Large corporate farms meet a great portion of the world's agricultural needs. Smaller private farms are important to maintain product and food diversity and availability. The main branches of agriculture include crop farming, dairy farming, ranching, poultry raising, and fruit growing.

What is the major agricultural product in your state?

How important is agriculture to your state's economy and identity?

```
B S B                 N B B
E S T H C O F W H A I E W T
K O A T F E F G V P L N I O D
C Y V B W R E T A C O R N S E O
S O W S R A C F P B T A T Y F H R
H F D H O H R I C E O F C A W Y G
T F L B E Y T L S H F R U I T H H
V E G E T A B L E R B I O W I O V
S E P U I V T E F Y L C P R B R T
H I O E H S F I A S K Y V B N S P
S L I C O T T O N G R O E T E R
C T R D Y S L R M S U G A R G
R N Y R B W N T W S B N N Y
  T A E U L D F T G F A O
  P P P H P L P B P F
  C I U O N O I N
  A O U G L
  F T L S R
  F T T W T
  U V R L U
  L N Y E E
  A B W C W
```

barley
bean
cattle
coffee
corn
cotton
fruit
hog
horse
oat
potato
poultry
rice
rye
sheep
soybean
sugar
vegetable
wheat

45

Mountains

Mountains are found all over the world, even under the oceans. Movements of the earth's surface, volcanoes, and erosion can create mountains. A mountainous area of land usually lies 2,000 feet above its surroundings.

Many plants and animals are found in mountain environments. Most mountains are cold, snow-covered, and rocky near the peaks. Padded hooves help some animals climb the jagged terrain. Many animals grow heavy fur to protect themselves from cold temperatures. Large forests near mountain bases provide food and shelter for a variety of plants and animals.

The Rocky Mountains are part of the Continental Divide. They separate rivers that flow east from rivers that flow west to the Pacific Ocean.

Notable U.S. Mountain Peaks

1. Mt. McKinley
Alaska
20, 320 ft

2. Mt. Whitney
California
14,495 ft

3. Mt. Ranier
Washington
14, 410 ft

4. Pikes Peak
Colorado
14,110 ft

5. Mauna Loa
Hawaii
13,677 ft

6. Borah Peak
Idaho
12,662 ft

7. Humphreys Peak
Arizona
12,633 ft

8. Mt. Hood
Oregon
11, 239 ft

9. Guadalupe Peak
Texas
8,749 ft

10. Mt. St. Helens
Washington
8,364 ft

11. Mt. Mitchell
North Carolina
6,684 ft

12. Mt. Washington
New Hampshire
6,288 ft

13. Mt. Rogers
Virginia
5,729 ft

14. Mt. Rushmore Nat'l Memorial
South Dakota
5,725 ft

15. Mt. Mansfield
Vermont
4,393 ft

Mount Rushmore National Memorial isn't a real mountain. The faces of four U.S. presidents are carved on a cliff.

```
A   R A
B V P D T N
C T G R P T Y U C
T H D U N A S M P D
R C P W S A K L I R I X
R A E F H D D L A T B K E
I A S D T M I E A P C H S E H
A U R C H I O D T Y L F H L L S O
B W N P A Y O R U A C I U W I W S P I
H R O E I D N Y E O T L B D P S A X K E M
S R I U R K E R I T N N V O R I E T N E Y A
E T R X Y A D T I E I O D R E U A N L R K U K
D V N C H S K R R W M A R H W L T O I N I
S I E R R A N E V A D A C E U G A C B A N
L O N D I G R E A T S M O K Y N O K H L N
V A   I O K D P L H E G   P G Y N O I
C H Y A         U C D A A
G E             R T T
```

Adirondack
Appalachian
Borah
Cascade
Great Smoky
Guadalupe
Mauna Loa

Pikes Peak
Ranier
Rocky
Rushmore
Sierra Nevada

Yaks climb as high as 20,000 feet in the Himalayan Mountains. That's higher than any other animal.

Major U.S. Mountain Ranges

Oceans and Seas

There are five oceans that surround the continents. Three of the great world oceans, in order of size, are the Pacific, the Atlantic, and the Indian. These three oceans meet around the continent of Antarctica in the Southern Hemisphere to form the Antarctic Ocean. These three oceans meet again at the top of the earth at the Arctic Ocean.

The word **sea** can name any body of water, from a large lake to an ocean. Connected to each ocean are smaller bodies of water called seas, bays, and gulfs that are defined by land or islands.

Think About It

Why are oceans and seas important to people?

Oceans cover over 70% of the earth and contain 97% of the world's water.

World Oceans

Arctic Ocean

Atlantic Ocean

Pacific Ocean

Pacific Ocean

Indian Ocean

Antarctic Ocean

The Dead Sea in Asia is so salty that nothing can live in it. Most seawater is 3.5% salt. The Dead Sea contains 24% salt.

The Marianas trench in the Pacific Ocean is the deepest place known on earth. It is 36,198 feet below sea level. Mt. Everest could fit inside of it.

48

```
            A T B E R N G
        L I B N O R T H Y T L A
      I L A R C T I C E K D R A C F O
    C E B R T N A T L A N T I C S I C H
    R H M E D I T E R R A N E A N F M P I N
    G Y G R R C I G A I I R W A D R I A T I C
    C A N I L H B E N E B T R I C Y H C N D B H
    E E N I T P A I B E B A L T I C I F I C O
    B G G H R N R H R D E T H N E F R T G
    K D A O T C I E I E Y A U D I I K N
    L W T F B D Y N L A T N I L C I K
    R M A N T A R C T I C B A P M T
    E B F C N T R I S G N N F A
    D       H C O C O C H I E O
            P I F O P A C F P
            A N R K N I A
            L B L A C K R
            C Y A T L S
            I C L F A
```

OCEANS

Antarctic

Arctic

Atlantic

Indian

Pacific

SEAS

Adriatic

Aegean

Baltic

Barents

Bering

Black

Caribbean

China

Coral

Mediterranean

North

Red

Tasman

SEE GLOSSARY · SEE GLOSSARY

49

Deserts

Deserts are regions that receive minimal rainfall. Deserts are also identified by the types of soil and vegetation that exist in an area. Most deserts are in warm climates, but the North Pole and South Pole can be considered deserts as well.

Deserts located in warm climates are the hottest places in the world. Some animals have adapted to the hot, dry conditions. They keep cool in the shade and can go for long periods of time without water. Their bodies are good at moving quickly over sand or burrowing into it.

Think About It

How do people protect themselves in hot climates?

World Deserts

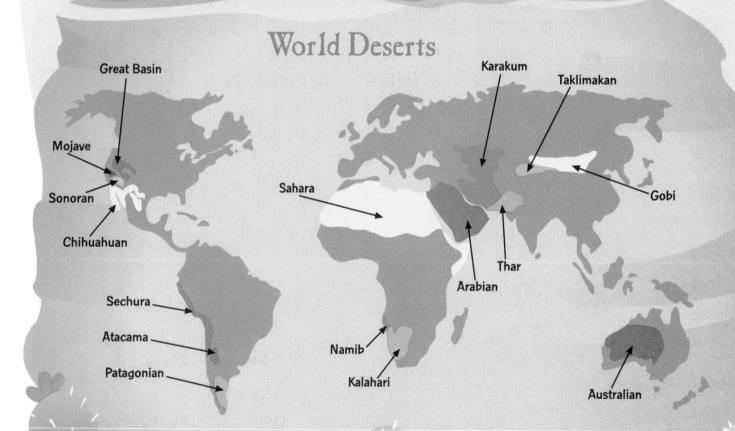

Great Basin
Mojave
Sonoran
Chihuahuan
Sechura
Atacama
Patagonian
Karakum
Taklimakan
Gobi
Sahara
Thar
Arabian
Namib
Kalahari
Australian

About 13% of the world's population lives in deserts. People protect themselves from the sun and heat with long clothing, tents, and adobe or mud homes.

An oasis is a place in the desert with enough water to support wells and springs.

The saguaro cactus can grow as tall as 60 feet. It is found only in parts of Arizona, California, and northwestern Mexico.

```
          G Y T A
          E V O I N A I B
          L L J B H W O J M S
          D P A I N T E D O T
          G Y S D E S R E J E
          B V A T A C A M A T H F
          G M B L Y H G Y T W A C
      S H   J H O I W N A M H K H M
    I P A Z   I P V J K R I R V Y J B I
    J T A R C   V A L W A U B L A D P M J
    U A H M K W S K T C N L V U I L U K A B
    I V L A U S T R A L I A N E N L Y I T I L
    M S K M R W N I G T V H M S H E C M A H
    P N W Y N T V G O H I A E I G Y J N D N
    T A R A B I A N I L R T O B E A I O
    N A T C P A I L Y I P A B V K S P
    J K A R A K U M Y S G A P T
          H N           T L E
          S W           T H S
          T             H Y
```

The mesquite tree's roots can reach over 260 feet deep to find water.

Arabian
Atacama
Australian
Death Valley
Gobi
Kalahari
Karakum
Mojave
Namib
Painted
Patagonian
Sahara
Thar

Camels are made for the desert. They can withstand heat, travel long distances, and go for days without water. Their hump is made of fat that can be used for energy. They can even clamp their nostrils and lips shut to keep out blowing sand.

Rivers

Rivers have always been important to people. Many major cities developed near rivers because they provided the chief form of transportation for trade, travel, and exploration. For centuries, farmers have found river valleys and plains to be especially fertile farmland.

Today, rivers provide electric power for industries. Dammed rivers store water for irrigation and turn turbines for electric generators. Fish and other wildlife depend on rivers for their unique habitats.

Think About It

What forms of recreation take place on rivers?

Amazon river dolphins are more agile and flexible than ocean dolphins.

World River Lengths (Miles)

Nile (Africa)	4,160
Amazon (South America)	4,000
Yangtze (Asia)	3,964
Congo (Africa)	2,900
Lena (Asia)	2,734
Mississippi (North America)	2,340
Missouri (North America)	2,315
Volga (Eastern Europe)	2,290
Yukon (North America)	1,979
Rio Grande (North America)	1,900
Danube (Europe)	1,776

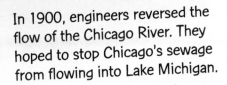

In 1900, engineers reversed the flow of the Chicago River. They hoped to stop Chicago's sewage from flowing into Lake Michigan.

If the Nile River could be placed in the United States, it would flow from California to the border between Virginia and West Virginia.

```
L H N S W Z I W O T I
C E Z V A L L E Y Y O
I N N P F U T N K P A
V K S S I R L A M I S S I S S I P P I C O L I
H O E M K O R M U L A M F Y P M Y K C T U N M
A D L N I N N I D T V S N N M I S S O U R I G
O A Y G T R I O G R A N D E N A Z O N I O L R
Y N N U A I U P T A E M P I H W Y E G D N E E
G U V K L V I T W A T U A P Z T G H O N Y C N
H B K N K E T R S R G I H Z T L I V B G H G C
C E C O L R D Z I R E V O Y O Y A N G T Z E S
T Y F B N B C H D T N Y I N A N H T U R I N T
```

Amazon	irrigation	Missouri	river	Yangtze
Congo	Lena	Nile	valley	Yukon
Danube	Mississippi	Rio Grande	Volga	

The Nile River is the world's longest river, but the Amazon River carries 200 times more water.

Natural Disasters

Natural disasters are sudden and extremely unfortunate events that affect many people. Meteorologists study weather and the earth to predict and understand natural disasters.

Different parts of the world are at risk for different natural disasters. In mountainous areas, avalanches are huge drifts of snow that rush downward. Volcanoes erupt hot gases and melted rock from miles below the earth's surface. Tornadoes, hurricanes, and typhoons are caused by tremendous winds. Earthquakes result from moving plates deep in the earth. Tsunamis are huge ocean waves caused by undersea earthquakes or volcanoes.

Use a word from the word search to label each type of natural disaster.

Hurricanes are called typhoons if they occur in the northwest Pacific Ocean. Near Australia and in the Indian Ocean they are called tropical cyclones.

_____

_____

_____   _____

Word list:
- avalanche
- blizzard
- earthquake
- flood
- hurricane
- meteorologist
- rock slide
- tornado
- tsunami
- typhoon
- volcano

SEE GLOSSARY · SEE GLOSSARY ·

Letter grid:

```
E A L O   N O K   Y U    U A Q   M A
B Y R O H U R R I C A N E T Y A I S U N A I N
C L C Y O N D C S V T Z V A B L I Z Z A R D M T R C
T F E D O I G I L N W R L C D V S M K X F R C Y H Y
S D O A Y O S T M E T E O R O L O G I S T R N P K E
U N R F R A G C W N Y F R C Z I D L H U N F T H F C
G G T I A T D T P G P U Q V K M T G C O I N G O A G
B L O A R S H O Y H N H I C H S Y F I A U H Y O H N
I I R U I U I Q R O N U V Z I F L O O D N X F N I
L Z N B C N C R U R O L O G Z E T I R S T O L E K
K Z A K Q A V A L A N C H E K A K C D O R G O I T
L Y D L N M W N L O K H N A Q L R Y L E M K D L
Q M O U E I U R R W C E M L K U O N T
N U N T S N       S T   B L I
U O E O K
S   N I
```

Experts sometimes cause avalanches on purpose. They use explosives to send snow down a mountain. This prevents the snow from building up and causing a more dangerous avalanche.

Universe

The universe includes everything that exists anywhere in space and time. It consists of all matter, light, and other forms of energy. The universe includes Earth, everything on Earth and within it, all of the planets, and everything in the solar system.

Scientists do not know the size of the universe. Many astronomers think that unusually bright, distant objects called quasars may be the farthest things from Earth in the universe. They may be as far as 10 billion light years away. There are different theories about the universe. One theory says that it is expanding. No one knows which theory, if any, is correct.

The Moon's near side always faces Earth and has been studied in detail. The Moon's far side always faces away from Earth. It was first photographed in 1959 by a Russian space probe.

The Milky Way Galaxy

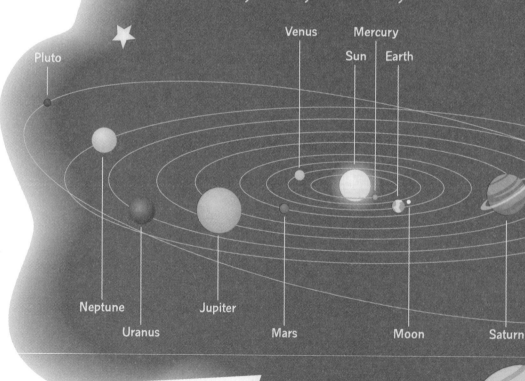

Pluto
Venus
Mercury
Sun
Earth
Neptune
Uranus
Jupiter
Mars
Moon
Saturn

The Hoba West Meteorite is the heaviest known meteorite. Weighing over 66 tons, it landed in southwest Africa.

The planet Saturn is known for its bright rings, which are made of ice.

astronomy

comet

galaxies

Jupiter

Mars

Mercury

Moon

planets

Saturn

stars

Sun

universe

Uranus

Venus

```
              J W X Y
        T E R B P V W A V T H
      M E V C W R E M U S Y N T C
    A R U S U N F U S A T U I D E S
    S R E S Q X S J E W Y R E R A V R V
    D A T W G T D M F T P V O S F A L X E F
    J X R Y N A E R E S U G N X A L N G R Y
    N Y A E H V G L N T J N C O M E T O U I T E
    M T P T L Y P X A N Y F I M X X F R N S U I
    P S L H N A O J U X R X T Y J N T K I S J T
    N O A S R E V O T K I N Y R A U E R V C K R
    M L N V X S J U P I T E R T C G P L E S X L
    T N E M E R S E L T S M S E V U H M R T A M
    Y T J E N H T U D N V O N E X A L S V U
    D S C S M U M E R C U R Y O M L N E I S
    R T Z B S S R T N X D V B O N C Y L
    Q A I T S T N V U D I O O X R T
    N R G E I J S A T U R N U M
    S S V U X L G S Y H C
          N T Q R S V
```

Help the shuttle find its way back to Earth.

Environments

Animals live all over the world, from frozen tundras to hot deserts. An animal's natural environment is called its habitat. Many animals migrate from one habitat to another. Other animals have adapted to their environment by developing special characteristics. For instance, heavy fur protects some animals from the cold.

Often, animals in similar habitats in different parts of the world have similar characteristics. For example, kangaroo rats in North America look like gerbils that live in the Sahara Desert.

Think About It

How do you think early humans adapted to different environments?

In what type of habitat do you live? How have you adapted?

```
L T A     R M A
A B R S H A D I U S A   S
  C N A R A I N F O R E S T C
D D W M O H F N E D O K T C W H D
N S E O E E W S C V G R E U A E O
G Y T U O D T F A B R F E F M P U F
C G W L N G D R G C T D N D S Y J M G E
D E P F T R A L I H C S D E V T H S N L
C I F I A C O R A L R E E F W R E C B A P
N U O S I S J O R N B H S R U Y I R W M Y J
V D G N W U K S Y D X E E N T M U K A O P
P O L A R I C E S M P L R B I A P B E L M I
T F M M X A G H L D W H T L C M Y L C Y M P
G B A S N C S T N S F T Y N O S W A M P C N
  L N M A R S H L A N D O R F B N I T D I
    H L C U L I P L R P D N N D P R A
        G A T A       W
        T U N D R A R
        A G S D O U
        I H R T
        N C S A
        K A T W
        H W S
```

Some plants and animals live outside their natural environments in zoos, aquariums, and botanical gardens.

coral reef
desert
forest
grassland
marshland
mountain
polar ice
rain forest
scrubland
swamp
tundra
woodland

SEE GLOSSARY · SEE GLOSSARY

Answers

Page 1

1. 5
2. 7
3. 2
4. 2

```
        Y W Y C K G
      P B R H R D A F L G
    T P A R A K E E T C O H
  W N I U V B S T Y D L C M
G L E S F H J B L P E D A E
U G U I N E A P I G V F N F
P H B V S A L B G T N I A P
P M A C A W K C S H M S R H
Y V F M O N K E Y C T H Y I
K W P B S L O V E B I R D J
A T U R T L E D N Z J N L
V M P L C E B W O T P M
  S Y M H O R S E G L
  H W N K V F J B
        A E
```

Page 2

```
              D K A S
            C G J B G L N U
          X M F W S X I C T Y S
        D L B K I J O F R S D C D
      W E G Y N S F H L A M V A
      P F C L V B A T V D F S T T
      M G K S Q E U B G P L F B U J
      U D M D O L P H I N R E W C
      S Y D R O C X I H M S X R H D
      J W A L R U S J T A K T M J O
      P J W R B S K M O N K E Y X R A K I
      X F L A K C E B N H T R L I H S P Y L
      R M S D O G L I V S K U N K M E E O
      Y A N S V F J D M G O A T H S C N
        H C L N              O D J
        P C U                R E P
        Y Q O Y              U E B
        R T O                H R
        A S G N              Y P W
```

Page 3

A. monkey
B. raccoon
C. dolphin
D. elephant
E. giraffe
F. bat
G. walrus
H. deer

Page 4

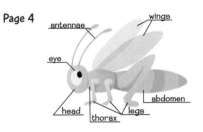

antennae, wings, eye, head, thorax, legs, abdomen

Page 5

```
          B C A M
        B F T M V I F I Y B
      B C U Y L G O U C Q C J H Y
    F D R C J G Y D S W A S P D B N
  L O N I V L R T E B Q T D I F U F T
  P E Y M C B H A E H V S U Y A S T J B
  G A N T K X K S D T E R F I F Y T T N M
  S B J H F E V F S T Y F G H Y T H E J K B
  T L C K M T Y N H X R B I L G K O R V D E
  V H D C O C K R O A C H U F D U J F N Y E
  N I S R T T G K P W F V H G J G K L F A K T
  W G H N H I F W P L Y C K M L A T Y P R H E
  P M B D I B U I E T J S M M A M D M I B U
  F C E B L S D R A G O N F L Y N Y W K C
  I Y T E R M I T E D E F E O U F G T I
  P B J T X T H P F V S T H T P L H Y
  M N S L H O D I L B I F B H J Y
  O Y D E L K A T Y D I D R
        S T F H R I F S K
```

Page 6

```
              A T B G C W K
          I G U A N A V G X U B H I C V
        V E V S F H S W C O E U L C S W R T C
      D I L T A I K D K D N A S C H L D N O S A H
    E M D E K L E S N I E F G I R K I F T A H E S
    F A L S A L A M A N D E R F J B O E R Y K J H
    G Q K I G I W H G K H G M O G T R S T O G E K
    H R T H Z G D E Y H G E K T G Y O T K E G X
    A U R J A N G R K W M V K B X I A R T Y
    N S A J C T R J C R O C O D I L E J D U G J I
    K W K T F G O K D Y P L D S T U H O K W R K H B
    B L F A M L R Y A Q F L H E O N L M L E T L F J T
    M T O R T O I S E J K Y N L W M E S F M L A M M R
    S U Y A B U J K          N M O T W N G E N F D
    O O Q O W A              I R H T H K I O H
```

Page 7

1. green tree frog
2. frilled lizard
3. tuatara
4. tailed frog
5. eft
6. rattlesnake

Page 8

```
H A
V E
B K R M P
L I M O E R
U N W J N
E G S H G
L J F T Q U J M
H A I S U I H O
W P Y S C V N I
N U T H A T C H B
V W O S E A G U L L
P H O L D R J W K P
C D G O M D T B X K M
D R O A D R U N N E R
W O O B F P F C O I B
K C P N B H P E I K L K
S J F A M I Y V C K G
J R T A N R N P I K C R E K D I
Q S G      D J O S T R I C H D W T E H D U O S
W U D L S D Q C Y S P A R R O W N A T I C R F V B L N T
  A H U M M I N G B I R D I S M Z N L N Y R B U H U O
  C V I H S N D T P G O L D F I N C H A J A Q O W L I
  W P E L I C A N      C K      F J M E L I J
```

Page 9

Page 10

```
                    D A T S G T A
                  U Q L R F K E L P H
                W J S H R I M P A J K I
                V F H H O N J M B W K D O
A                 E S V K A N C S M P E B O
F C               F H H L C K L A T E Q E F L
D A R A B G D S E A H O R S E J O A D T P
O M H A S Q U I D R H R M Q P U K P F J H
B T Y B I V H J K S A I L F I S H U A I
J B A R N A C L E P L A N K T O N J S N
C G K J K S O G M E Q S T A R F I S H V
L O H A          S T L T E Q H O N Q U I
S M D            S E A A N E M O N E
T
```

Page 11

Page 12

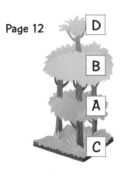

D
B
A
C

Page 13

```
T W
O L R        H M O T
H Y E C A P Y B A R A
E M A R M O S E T N A R
T L L G O U Y U R D N S Y
V A E F O P R L T R G I J
G O J P P A R R O T I U E W
H N K S I H U I H U L T R L
T O U C A N R A C L N L A I K
F S C O R P I O N J L O N S
K R L C X M I C G T F A I B
E L E O P A R D P O K L R
H V B T A M A R I N M M
N J R Y H C U S C U S
G A      G R
```

Page 14

```
            S A
          B R V W
    A Z Q K M A Y F L Y C T J C
  D O F U B J N O M D B H T D T Z
A E E S E T H C H E E T A H B W E A
Q F H X F T H T K Q N F S M W F N C T L
G U A O G Z R G B K U T R E L G Q P S T
P V H M W A H I S R E T Z L S T H L R H
I D T B O L N X C I R K T E H Y D A J O I
H J P N U G Q E K J H O Q Y O I N Z T P J G
L V K I S A H U R T B K G T N K C W Y K H L
J P A R R O T L M M V K L I X B L C P J L N
L W M V T A M A G T O I B U R M S K U N K
N B R O P N H R K L N D N Y A T H S N C
U W S F O H H K A N G K O D W F T F O
T D O L P W A L V C F E P R S F P J
  T K Q E U J U P O I H Y Q K T E
    K X R A T Y R B M R P L R
      I F H H S R H S T O
          F T A
```

Page 15

1. parrot
2. cheetah
3. quetzal
4. ostrich
5. piranha
6. flea
7. howler monkey
8. chameleon
9. platypus

Page 16

```
                        T B O H
                      C C O I C
            R T Y R A N N O S A U R U S N D
          S Y U E E A J E X T I N C T R J E K
        X F A T H P O Y F P F O S S I L G S
      F Q R T P X F Y T R I C E R A T O P S
    M V L O S A F R W S I A T L O T J X T I
  P A L E O N T O L O G Y L P S L R Q N
B R A C H I O S A U R U S E T Y U
D E V U A B R S H J Y I N C T K O
L S T E G O S A U R U S B I    R
G A L L O S A U R U S M
N I U Y O E N R H Y R
H A D R O S A U R W
      V S O N
      J R
```

Page 17

```
            P T C S Y
        L B U B L H K
    G H O S M I E L C
  N O I J A H P Y A N
E S G E N F P S F T C
M R H V D T E N N I S
C H B C A G R R G D E
O S U T L Z S H S V C
Z T I S O G Y N X
W T E J B G H O D
T O V E A K S W F
A N O B L C L S J
P K M D L T A H
T S K N G E W O O
B H N T W T N H E
M O C C A S I N S
E O F Q L K Q
S M T S J D
G R S C
```

Page 18

```
        T N A   V A M T      D T N
      A R R E M   N T L Q J   B A S Y
    B P W O S C X C I T E H K D S T L O
  D G O E A V O C A D O F E B F P I F M D
  K B R V P R E H B G V J R K E A K B J H
  F O M X C B P J Y B L O F A S J R E G E Y K
  S X V I S A C E H A X C N B R N A F E X E M
Y T D C R K F U L R G H A K I P W G C H Z Y T
L A I E I N T C L H E I G D V O I U A T U K P
D K M L T G M U F I J N T G R T N S F R C A J
S H P E A M K M V U F C D Y D A N R J C C S M
O I N R F B L B T G D L T I L T D C H O H Z L
X C M Y E C J E M U P S O H X O B I M R I U H
    X A R N W R T B W G N F G S N N A N
      O R C I G N O B E A N K I H I O
        P R D H Y I J W R Y N
          W V O H I M P B Z H
            L S H T R K V
              X M O
```

Page 19

```
        N W A I C
      M C D N J H B
    S K E H M L E S O
  D O C S L X W R P Y N
  E L S W A O T R F V I
  S I G T P B N Y K G O
  R V D T R M I V N R J T
  E O N I A C H L H T H U
  B I R C G W A T P W K I T V P G I
  M P O I J B O J L P L C G O K M O L H P G
  D A T E R C E F G U K E N V R Q F L I E N B
W Y P N T L P N R H I M L M J B A N A N A C Y
L M A H G Y I M U R T E M U O R T N R K C D I
I G Y C W O N K F J Y U N B P N H W G U H N X
M U A Y X R E W T G I P R G R A P E F E H O I
E G P K U T A P L R A S P B E R R Y H N L D
E A P P L E X H O V B T O V P F G M I
Y R G R T R P G R A P E F R U I T I
  W C H B L U E B E R R Y W A T O G
    E T J E N W K A J F T V H
      R E T S A F R U
```

Page 20

```
              T A
          Y P V C C N B
      P P I E D P I P E R V
    G U T D T S F K N I S L U D
  R I S T H E L E S T D N K W H E
  A S F D R E T R P S E O D H L
  B I K G R E T J R G L R C I G
  H N R F A P E D O P S H E C L
  I B V T B I S L B U X A W L H I
  O P D B N U G I J Y N H Y L I P
  O K E I G L A N T C S I K M A O
  T J L T B Y X H S T E N K G W V
  S B M T E H F O V M L R P O B M
  L T G A R G O Y U A E N L H S N
  H E S U I P D X B N A P D T R S
  W P T K P A V N D W C I P L T
  Q W Y T M C N T G O J L G I
  R O H X R B R D R Z C O R S
  C S I T G S F E A S C T
  S N O W W H I T E R K
  X B R V T N U E M I S
    L N V J L
```

Page 21

1. Pinocchio
2. Robin Hood
3. Cinderella
4. Snow White
5. Three Little Pigs
6. Peter Rabbit
7. Hansel and Gretel
8. Goldilocks
9. Peter Pan
10. Sleeping Beauty
11. Pied Piper
12. Puss in Boots

Page 22

```
          G A T M A U S P
    M R B U W Z S T B N G B O K
    I W C A N D E R S E N C W Y D
      T I L H B N T D W M R I K R
  Y N K E T I D N Y L M B L S E
    B U J S N O A F Y A E M D N F
    D K O L E H W K B G M O N E G K
      L L W A U M V O J E L H H R H
      K O C B H S I R S L U N M O D
    J B A L K B S T J M B C T K O B
    M E T E Y E N T C A E I N S K I
    V L K A B L W L I N D G R E N L
    E O Y O M H P N U S T D E I O R
    A N L G N T S K O N V N F H S N
    X O K A O T H W R I Y T G F T I
    P V T E C W E P H K S R Y N S R
    S Y N G A I D Y M I L N E M O X
    R W P O T T E R R T F U G R
      G E A H N S G I R S E
        H N T E P U H
          E S R U H Y
            N P M
```

Page 23

1. Potter
2. Twain
3. Sendak
4. Seuss
5. Andersen
6. Lobel
7. Lindgren
8. Milne
9. Keats
10. White
11. Wilder
12. Bemelmans

Pages 24–25

String: cello, guitar, harp, violin

Wind: bugle, clarinet, flute, oboe, saxophone, trombone, trumpet, tuba

Percussion: cymbals, drum, gong, triangle

Keyboard and Electronic: organ, piano, synthesizer

```
          H L S T C T N A I K
        M J B V I O L I N L C S B
      N O C E L L O A G K C D Y I U C
      F U S V I D K M R N R H O N M N K
      C E A F A P J T R I G W E L T S B I P
      F P G O N G X L F H N T A Y S H T Z A F T
      T O S P H C G O N T E V H N T E G U G L K
      F R H Y U S I B P G T R T W H S R J Y U S
O R G U I T A R O U H H U C I P I A N O T C E
J H B N M R G S B T W O J B A L Z F U D E F J
T H A K N P F U O T R E N U A T E H C M S K V
L R U W E T E F A I D E I D R U M B L C
C Y P O H T R V D T A B M O T      T M
O T            W O S R E N C S N
        P M O B U G L E Z
        R B C L P L Y N
        T O F S T E
        D R N Y I
        S U G E S
        W Y P T
```

Page 26

```
              B A A
        T Y P E W R I T E R
      X L J S C M U K O P F L
    D R A H C T P D S H R B O N C
    E T W S C E O E Y I N I T E I O
  K G R B E T L J S A F K N C L M T T
  Y T A I R P L A N E M N T S E Y T E
  T O H D P K O O H O B D E I W C J O L A
  A R D I G U N P O W D E R N S T X N E Y
  W P A O B T W H J T G O N G G R K G G T
  D T S C F N Y A F R H M J P L I J I R L
  E R M O T I O N P I C T U R E C N N A
  G M J I O M E F U P O Y E H L M E P
  X H N V X R A Y O T T J S G I A I H
  R B P O F K T H P C T S H G X R
  A Y L T E L E P H O N E H P
    C O M P U T E R H Y T
    W G T P S R T
```

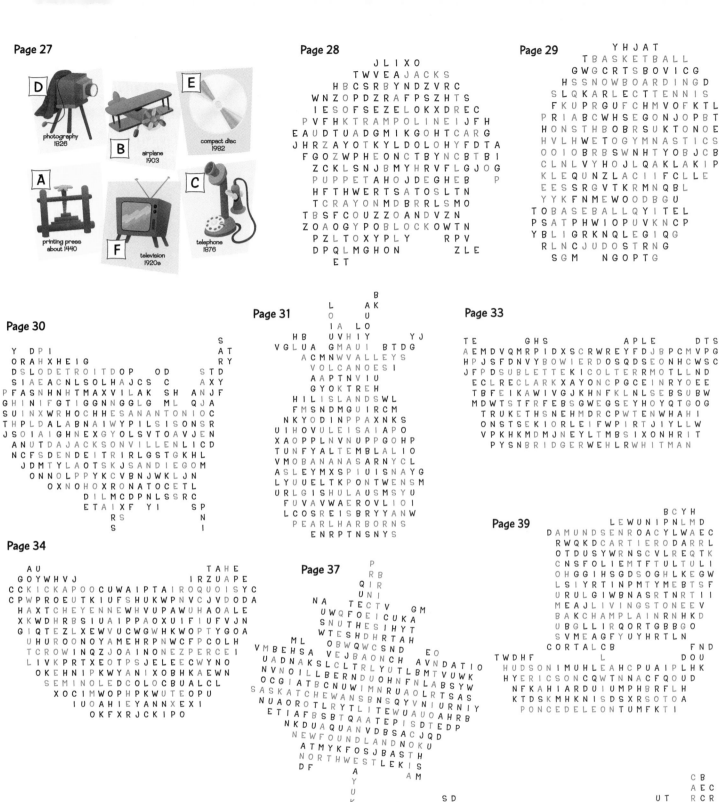

Page 43

```
          N C                     E U A
        Y H         T S Y P W H J V B
    C G I R U Y L P C N W S C N M K T
    N K J Y O E L A G R A N D C A N Y O N S C
  S C T M R W A L R D C E R A E N Y K E O H G U
F Y O S E M I T E B L H F K D S D L A F N E
I W N G I A L S V F G S O G L D W A E D R T W E G L
H X G O S D Y N I A L H B V W H E B O L Y M P I C Y M O H
L   N L O I E V E R G L A D E S A E T O B I H
  S C A N Y O N L A N D S A G T I K Y D E
  H A N C E S A C U K C H O R H O N L K X
  E   G   I V H F G L A U S N V Y N L
      E N E A M V E A C A V R E
      R Y N L E A G W L H J N
      V M A R N U S L O K
      A P C N V A T E Y G
      D Y U S D R O Y S
      E C V R O E O D
      S N H G X A N R
      T O A C H D H O
      B A D L A N D S
      G Y V O I S S V
      V L R W A N B A
      E N O M I
```

Page 44

```
C V E A P T I S W P U C H U R C H
A S Y K Y N P I L B E O T C T
F T O W E R W A Q E L S V I S
I N H D L V A D G W R P G O Y
U A E M J P N M S O E I H C N L S K E
L R K Y X L N K I A D T O D A I V W Y
S H W G C A T H E D R A L V G B D E H
H K T H G N G O R A F L C N O R I R
D I Y U S E F B M T I U H U G A V N
Y V R S V T P Y E H M P A C U R S T
N K E B C A A M T O O S L A E Y N M
R Y T D E R L D O Y G T L S O L C
B R S T M I A E I D O O E T W D G
N A N H E U N P B U E I N L P I A
P L G E O M I S E J M O O E T U
V Y O D U S P M I R U D S P P A
K L N Q C R S L D G S B N M T Y
P T R U H Y U F E A E R V E N
L H O U S E M O S Q U E T M S
A L X M T M L Y P R M Y C E T
V C P R B K P O N S B K T H P
```

Page 45

```
        B S B           N B B
      E S T H C O F W H A I E W T
      K O A T F E F G V P L N I O D
      C Y V B W R E T A C O R N S E O
    S O W S R A C F P B T A T Y F H R
    H F D H O H R I C E O F C A W Y G
    T F L B E Y T L S H F R U I T H H
    V E G E T A B L E R B I O W I O V
    S E P U I V T E F Y L C P R B R T
    H I O E H S F I A S K Y V B N S P
    S L I C O T T O N G R O E T E R
    C T R D Y S L R M S U G A R G
    R N Y R B W N T W S B N N Y
    T A E U L D F T G F A O
    P P P H P L P B P F
    C I U O N O I N
    A O U G L
    F T L S R
    F T T W T
    U V R L U
    L N Y E E
    A B W C W
```

Page 47

```
        A   R A
      B V P D T N
    C T G R P T Y U C
    T H D U N A S M P D
  R C P W S A K L I R I X
  R A E F H D D L A T B K E
  I A S D T M I E A P C H S E H
A U R C H I O D T Y L F H L L S O
B W N P A Y O R U A C I U W I W S P I
H R O E I D N Y E O T L B D P S A X K E M
S R I U R K E R I T N N V O R I E T N E Y A
E T R X Y A D T I E I O D R E U A N L R K U K
D V N C H S K R R W M A R H W L T O I N I
S I E R R A N E V A D A C E U G A C B A N
L O N D I G R E A T S M O K Y N O K H L N
V A   I O K D P L H E G   P G Y N O I
    C H Y A           U C D A A
    G E               R T T
```

Page 49

```
          A T B E R N G
      L I B N O R T H Y T L A
    I L A R C T I C E K D R A C F O
  C E B R T N A T L A N T I C S I C H
  R H M E D I T E R R A N E A N F M P I N
G Y G R R C I G A I I R W A D R I A T I C
C A N I L H B E N E B T R I C Y H C N D B H
E E N I T P A I B E B A L T I C I F I C O
B G G H R N R H R D E T H N E F R T G
K D A O T C I E I E Y A U D I I K N
L W T F B D Y N L A T N I L C I K
R M A N T A R C T I C B A P M T
E B F C N T R I S G N N F A
D   H C O C O C H I E U
    P I F O P A C F P
    A N R K N I A
    L B L A C K R
    C Y A T L S
    I C L F A
```

Page 51

```
              G Y T A
            E V O I N A I B
          L L J B H W O J M S
          D P A I N T E D O T
          G Y S D E S R E J E
          B V A T A C A M A T H F
          G M B L Y H G Y T W A C
        S H   J H O I W N A M H K H M
    I P A Z   I P V J K R I R V Y J B I
  J T A R C   V A L W A U B L A D P M J
U A H M K W S K T C N L V U I L U K A B
I V L A U S T R A L I A N E N L Y I T I L
M S K M R W N I G T V H M S H E C M A H
P N W Y N T V G O H I A E I G Y J N D N
T A R A B I A N I L R T O B E A I O
N A T C P A I L Y I P A B V K S P
J K A R A K U M Y S G A P T
    H N               T L E
    S W               H S
    T                 Y
```

Page 53

```
        L H N S W Z I W O T I
        C E Z V A L L E Y Y O
        I N N P F U T N K P A
V K S S I R L A M I S S I S S I P P I C O L I
H O E M K O R M U L A M F Y P M Y K C T U N M
A D L N I N N I D T V S N N M I S S O U R I G
O A Y G T R I O G R A N D E N A Z O N I O L R
Y N N U A I U P T A E M P I H W Y E G D N E E
G U V K L V I T W A T U A P Z T G H O N Y C N
H B K N K E T R S R G I H Z T L I V B G H G C
C E C O L R D Z I R E V O Y O Y A N G T Z E S
T Y F B N B C H D T N Y I N A N H T U R I N T
```

Page 54
Clockwise from top:
tornado, tsunami, flood, earthquake

Page 55
Clockwise from top:
volcano, blizzard, rock slide

```
E A L O   N O K   Y U   U A Q   M A
B Y R O H U R R I C A N E T Y A I S U N A I N
C L C Y O N D C S V T Z V A B L I Z Z A R D M T R C
T F E D O I G I L N W R L C D V S M K X F R C Y H Y
S D O A Y O S T M E T E O R O L O G I S T R N P K E
U N R F R A G C W N Y F R C Z I D L H U N F T H F C
G G T I A T D T P G P U Q V K M T G C O I N G O A G
B L O A R S H O Y H N H I C H S Y F I A U H Y O H N
I I R U I U I Q R O N U V Z I F L O O D N X F N I
L Z N B C N C R U R O L O G Z E T I R S T O L E K
K Z A K Q A V A L A N C H E K A K C D O R G O I T
L Y D L N M W N L O K H N A Q L R Y L E M K D L
Q M O U E I U R R W C E M L K U O N T
N U N T S N       S T   B L I
U O E O K
S   N I
```

Page 57

```
            J W X Y
          T E R B P V W A V T H
        M E V C W R E M U S Y N T C
      A R U S U N F U S A T U I D E S
      S R E S Q X S J E W Y R E R A V R V
    D A T W G T D M F T P V O S F A L X E F
    J X R Y N A E R E S U G N X A L N G R Y
    N Y A E H V G L N T J N C O M E T O U I T E
    M T P T L Y P X A N Y F I M X X F R N S U I
    P S L H N A O J U X R X T Y J N T K I S J T
    N O A S R E V O T K I N Y R A U E R V C K R
    M L N V X S J U P I T E R T C G P L E S X L
    T N E M E R S E L T S M S E V U H M R T A M
    Y T J E N H T U D N V O N E X A L S V U
    D S C S M U M E R C U R Y O M L N E I S
    R T Z B S S R T N X D V B O N C Y L
    Q A I T S T N V U D I O O X R T
    N R G E I J S A T U R N U M
    S S V U X L G S Y H C
    N T Q R S V
```

Page 58

```
        L T A     R M A
      A B R S H A D I U S A   S
      C N A R A I N F O R E S T C
    D D W M O H F N E D O K T C W H D
    N S E O E E W S C V G R E U A E O
    G Y T U O D T F A B R F E F M P U F
    C G W L N G D R G C T D N D S Y J M G E
    D E P F T R A L I H C S D E V T H S N L
    C I F I A C O R A L R E E F W R E C B A P
    N U O S I S J O R N B H S R U Y I R W M Y J
    V D G N W U K S Y D X E E N T M U K A O P
    P O L A R I C E S M P L R B I A P B E L M I
    T F M M X A G H L D W H T L C M W L C Y M P
    G B A S N C S T N S F T Y N O S W A M P C N
    L N M A R S H L A N D O R F B N I T D I
    H L C U L I P L R P D N N D P R A
        G A T A     W
        T U N D R A R
        A G S D O U
        I H R T
        N C S A
        K A T W
        H W S
```

Glossary

Use a dictionary to learn about vocabulary words that aren't defined in this glossary.

abdomen: tail end of an insect.

Adriatic Sea: part of the Mediterranean Sea between Italy and the Balkan Peninsula.

Aegean Sea: part of the Mediterranean Sea between Greece and Turkey.

allosaurus: meat-eating dinosaur with big, curved teeth. It walked on two legs.

amateur: sport played for pleasure rather than payment.

Amundsen, Roald: an explorer who led the first expedition to the South Pole.

Anchorage: the largest city in Alaska.

antennae: feelers on the head of an insect.

Apache: southwestern Native Americans.

apatosaurus: huge plant-eating dinosaur with a long neck and an arched back.

Appleseed, Johnny: the nickname of John Chapman, a pioneer who planted apple trees in Ohio and Indiana.

Armstrong, Neil: the first person to step on the moon.

avalanche: snow drifts in mountainous areas that rush downward.

Badlands: a national park in South Dakota with ravines, cliffs, and prehistoric fossils.

Baltic Sea: a sea in northern Europe.

Barents Sea: part of the Arctic Ocean near northeast Europe.

barnacle: shellfish that attaches itself to boats, rocks, and other animals.

Bering Sea: part of the north Pacific Ocean, north of the Aleutian Islands.

Black Sea: a sea between Europe and Asia.

blizzard: a severe winter storm with dry driving snow, strong winds, and intense cold.

boccie: game that is like lawn bowling.

Boone, Daniel: a pioneer who explored the Appalachians and cleared the Wilderness Road.

Bowie, James: a pioneer from Texas. He invented the bowie knife and fought in the battle at Alamo.

brachiosaurus: tall plant-eating dinosaur with a long neck and a massive sloping body.

Bridger, Jim: a pioneer who was a hunter, trapper, fur trader, and guide in the Rocky Mountains and Utah.

Cabot, John: an explorer who completed the first English voyage to North America.

canopy: top layer of rain forest trees.

Canyonlands: a national park in Utah with canyons, mesas, and 1,000-year-old Native American rock carvings.

capybara: largest living rodent. It looks like a large guinea pig with no tail and webbed feet.

Caribbean Sea: part of the Atlantic Ocean near Central and South America.

caribou: a large reindeer.

Carlsbad Caverns: a national park in New Mexico with underground caves.

Carson, Kit: a pioneer who led government officials along the Oregon Trail.

Cartier, Jacques: a French navigator who explored Canada.

cartilage: strong elastic tissue that connects bones and forms human ears and noses.

castle: a fortified residence, usually for royalty or the wealthy in medieval times.

cathedral: a principal Christian church.

cello: large string instrument that is played with a bow and rests on the ground.

cellophane: clear plastic used as a food covering and as tape.

Champlain, Samuel de: a French explorer who founded the city of Quebec in Canada.

Cherokee: southeastern Native Americans.

Cheyenne: Native Americans of the northern Plains.

China Sea: part of the Pacific Ocean near China.

Chippewa: northeastern Native Americans.

church: a building for public Christian worship.

cicada: insect that makes a loud, shrill sound.

clarinet: wind instrument played by blowing across a reed in the mouthpiece.

Clark, William: a pioneer who journeyed with Meriwether Lewis to explore the Louisiana Territory and the Pacific Northwest.

cobra: large poisonous snake that spreads its skin like a hood when agitated.

cockroach: insect with a flattened body that is a household pest.

cod: fish found in the Atlantic Ocean.

cold-blooded: animals, such as reptiles and fish, whose body temperatures change according to their surroundings.

Colter, John: a pioneer who joined the Lewis and Clark expedition in 1803.

Columbus, Christopher: an Italian explorer who helped establish European links to the Western Hemisphere.

continental shelf: shallow area of the ocean floor along the coast.

coral: hard material made of the skeletons of tiny sea animals.

coral reef: a ridge of rocks and coral found mostly in warm, shallow tropical seas.

Coral Sea: part of the Pacific Ocean near Australia.

Cortés, Hernando: a Spanish explorer who conquered what is now central and southern Mexico.

cotton gin: machine for separating the cotton fibers from the seeds.

Crockett, Davy: a famous hunter, scout, soldier, and congressman. He died in the battle at Alamo.

croquet: outdoor game that uses mallets to hit wooden balls through wire hoops in the ground.

Crow: Native Americans of the northern Plains.

cuscus: possum that is most active at night.

Death Valley: a national park in California and Nevada. This desert is the lowest land surface in the U.S.

Denali: a national park in Alaska with Mt. McKinley, the highest mountain in North America.

desert: an area that has very little rainfall.

Donner, George and Jacob: pioneers who tried to lead 82 settlers through the Sierra Nevadas. They became snowbound in the winter of 1846–1847.

dragonfly: insect with two sets of wings and a long, slender body.

Drake, Sir Francis: the first Englishman to sail around the world.

earthquake: a series of vibrations caused by movements in the earth's crust.

emergent trees: very tall trees that grow above the top layer of a rain forest.

eoraptor: small meat-eating dinosaur that walked on two legs.

Ericson, Leif: a Norse explorer who led the first European expedition to North America in about A.D. 1000. He was Eric the Red's son.

Eric the Red: the nickname of the Norse explorer Eric Thorvaldson. He colonized Greenland.

Everglades: a national park in Florida that is a subtropical wilderness.

extinct: refers to a type of animal or plant that has died out. None are living today.

fiction: invented or imagined story about people and places that are not real.

flood: a flowing of water on land that is not normally submerged.

floor: dark ground of a rain forest.

flute: wind instrument played by blowing across a hole at one end and covering holes to change the tones.

forest: an area covered with trees and underbrush, also called a woodland.

fossil: remains of a plant or an animal from millions of years ago preserved as a rock.

gecko: small tropical lizard that is usually active at night.

glacier: a large mass of ice that moves slowly across a continent.

Glacier: a national park in Montana with glaciers and lakes.

gong: percussion instrument that is a metal disk that makes a hollow, echoing sound when struck.

Grand Canyon: a national park in Arizona. The Colorado River cut the one-mile-deep canyon.

grassland: an area where most of the vegetation is grasses, sometimes called a prairie.

guppy: tiny freshwater fish that is a common pet.

habitat: plant or animal's natural environment.

hadrosaur: common duck-billed plant-eating dinosaurs.

Haida: Native Americans of the northwest coast.

harp: large triangular string instrument that is played by plucking the strings.

heron: bird that lives near water and has long, thin legs and a long beak.

Hillary, Sir Edmund Percival: a New Zealand man who reached the top of Mount Everest and returned.

Honolulu: the capital of Hawaii.

Hudson, Henry: an English explorer who tried to find a water route across North America.

hula: a native Hawaiian dance.

hurricane: a violent tropical storm in the Atlantic Ocean with high winds and rain.

Inuit: Native Americans of Alaska and northern Canada.

invertebrate: animal without a backbone.

Iroquois: northeastern Native Americans.

jacana: small tropical bird with long toes for walking on water plants.

Jemison, Mary: a woman whose family was captured by Native Americans and French soldiers. She became a member of the Seneca tribe.

judo: sport in which two people use quick movements to try to throw each other to the ground.

Juneau: the capital of Alaska.

katydid: green insect resembling a grasshopper. The male rubs its front wings to make a shrill noise.

kayak: a small boat propelled by hand with a paddle.

kelp: large, edible, brown seaweed.

Kickapoo: northeastern Native Americans.

kingfisher: small bird that lives near water and has bright feathers and a long bill.

Kwakiutl: Native Americans of the northwest coast.

lemur: small mammal resembling a monkey that lives mainly in trees.

Lewis, Meriwether: a pioneer who journeyed with William Clark to explore the Louisiana Territory and the Pacific Northwest.

limpet: sea animal with a protective shell. It clamps to rocks with a muscular foot.

Livingstone, David: an English explorer who was the first European to see many parts of Africa.

luge: one- or two-person sled for racing down a chute.

macaw: large parrot with colorful feathers and a loud voice.

Magellan, Ferdinand: a Portuguese explorer who captained the first voyage around the world.

mandrill: large baboon. The male has a ribbed blue and red face.

marmoset: small monkey with a long tail.

Marquette, Jacques: a French missionary who explored the upper Mississippi River and the Midwest.

marshland: an area with marshes, swamps, bogs, and other low, wet land.

mayfly: insect with delicate wings.

McLoughlin, John: a Canadian-born trader called the "Father of Oregon."

Mediterranean Sea: a sea between Europe, Africa, and Asia.

meteorologist: a scientist who studies weather and the earth.

mosque: a Muslim temple or place of worship.

mountain: an area with a much higher elevation than its surroundings.

museum: a building where works of art, scientific specimens, or other valuable objects are stored and displayed.

mushers: people who compete in dogsled races.

myna: dark brown bird that can imitate the human voice.

Navajo: southwestern Native Americans.

Nez Perce: Native Americans of the Plateau area.

North Sea: part of the Atlantic Ocean between Great Britain and the European mainland.

nuthatch: small bird with a short tail and a sharp beak.

oboe: wind instrument played by blowing across a double reed in the mouthpiece.

okapi: mammal that resembles a giraffe but with a much shorter neck and striped legs.

Olympic: a national park in Washington with ocean, mountain, and rain forest habitats.

orangutan: large ape with long, reddish-brown hair and long, strong arms.

organ: keyboard instrument with one or more keyboards and pipes of different lengths.

pagoda: a temple or sacred building usually found in Asia.

paleontology: study of fossils and ancient life forms, including dinosaurs.

papayas: large yellow melonlike fruit.

Pearl Harbor: a U.S. naval base in Hawaii. Japanese forces attacked Pearl Harbor during World War II.

piranha: fish that eats other fish and sometimes larger animals that enter the water.

planetarium: a building that uses moving projectors to display stars, planets, and other visible objects in space.

plankton: tiny animals and plants that float in bodies of water.

platypus: egg-laying mammal with webbed feet and a broad bill, from Australia.

polar ice: the layer of ice at the North or South Pole.

polo: game in which two teams of four players on horseback use long mallets to hit a small ball.

Polo, Marco: an Italian trader who explored central Asia and China. His journey to China and back took 24 years.

Pomo: Native Americans of what is now California.

Ponce de León, Juan: a Spanish explorer who led the first Europeans into Florida. He also conquered Puerto Rico.

Pueblo: southwestern Native Americans.

pyramid: a building shaped like a pyramid. Most pyramids were tombs or temple platforms.

quetzal: bird with red and green feathers. The male has very long tail feathers.

rain forest: a tropical forest with high annual rainfall.

Red Sea: part of the Indian Ocean between Africa and Arabia.

Redwood: a national park in California with the world's largest living tree.

roadrunner: small bird with brown or black feathers and a long tail. It runs quickly on the ground.

rock slide: when a mass of rocks suddenly dislodges and falls.

Saguaro: a national park in Arizona with a cactus forest that includes large saguaro cacti.

saxophone: brass wind instrument with keys for the fingers.

scrubland: an area covered with low trees and shrubs.

sea anemone: sea animal with a tube-shaped body and circles of tentacles around its mouth.

sea fan: colorful coral with a flat fanlike shape.

Seminole: southeastern Native Americans.

Shawnee: northeastern Native Americans.

Shenandoah: a national park in Virginia with the Blue Ridge Mountains and Skyline Drive.

Sioux: Native Americans of the northern Plains.

skink: lizard with flat, overlapping, smooth scales.

skyscraper: a tall building usually used for offices.

sloth: mammal with long legs, curved claws, and shaggy fur. It moves slowly and hangs upside down in trees.

Smith, Jebediah: a fur trader who established trade routes to California and the Northwest.

Soto, Hernando de: a Spanish explorer who helped defeat the Incan empire and led the first Europeans to the Mississippi River.

squash: game played by two people who use racquets to hit a small rubber ball against the walls of an enclosed court.

stadium: a sports arena with tiers of seats for spectators.

stegosaurus: plant-eating dinosaur with two rows of spines down its back and long, heavy spikes on its tail.

Sublette, William: a fur trader who named a shortcut through the Rocky Mountains called Sublette's Cutoff.

swamp: an area of wet, spongy land.

synagogue: a Jewish temple or place of worship.

synthesizer: electronic instrument that can make a variety of sounds and imitate other instruments.

tamarin: mammal that resembles a monkey with a long tail and silky fur.

tapir: large animal that looks like a pig with a long snout and hooves.

tarsier: small mammal that resembles a monkey with large eyes and padded fingers and toes.

Tasman Sea: part of the Pacific Ocean between Australia and New Zealand.

telegraph: device that sends messages over long distances by using a code of electrical signals.

temple: a place for religious worship.

termite: insect that eats wood and resembles an ant.

thorax: part of an insect's body between its head and its abdomen.

titi: small red or gray monkey.

tomb: a place where a person is buried or a building that is a memorial to a dead person.

tornado: a violent windstorm that can be identified by a long funnel-shaped cloud that extends to the ground.

toucan: brightly colored tropical bird with a large beak.

tower: a vertical part of a building that is much taller than the building around it, sometimes a prison or fortress.

triangle: triangular percussion instrument that is struck with a metal rod.

triceratops: plant-eating dinosaur with a short frill behind its head and three horns.

trombone: brass wind instrument with a long bent tube that slides back and forth to play different tones.

tsunami: huge ocean waves caused by undersea earthquakes or volcanoes.

tuatara: large reptile that looks like a lizard. It can live over 100 years.

tuba: large brass wind instrument that makes a deep sound. It has several valves to change the tones.

tundra: an extremely cold and dry area. Part of the soil is frozen all year.

typhoon: a violent tropical storm in the Pacific Ocean or China seas with high winds and rain.

tyrannosaurus: large meat-eating dinosaur that walked on two legs.

understory: middle layer of trees in a rain forest.

violin: string instrument with four strings that are played with a bow.

volcano: a vent in the earth's crust that allows lava, steam, and ash to come out.

warm-blooded: animals, such as mammals and birds, whose body temperatures must remain constant.

Whitman, Marcus: an American pioneer, doctor, and missionary in what is now the Pacific Northwest.

woodland: an area covered with trees, also called a forest.

Ute: Native Americans of the Great Basin area.

Yellowstone: a national park in Idaho, Montana, and Wyoming. It has the world's greatest geyser area.

Yosemite: a national park in California with mountain scenery, including gorges and waterfalls.